About the aut

Calum Nicholas is the Senior Power Unit Assembly Technician at Red Bull Racing, and is responsible for ensuring the various F1 systems are operating and optimal for each race. Calum also forms part of the all-important crew that up until 2023 held the world record for a Formula One pitstop.

Since joining Red Bull Racing in 2015, Calum has been part of the team that has returned Red Bull to its winning ways. Red Bull have won four consecutive World Championships with driver Max Verstappen, and in 2022 and 2023 won the Constructors' Championship.

LIFE IN THE PITLANE

MY JOURNEY TO THE HEART OF F1

Calum Nicholas

PIATKUS

PIATKUS

First published in Great Britain in 2025 by Piatkus

1 3 5 7 9 10 8 6 4 2

A CIP catalogue record for this book
is available from the British Library.

ISBN: 978-0-34944-343-0 (hardback)
978-0-34944-344-7 (paperback)

Photographs from pages 1–7 of plate section from the author's collection;
photographs on page 8 by Mark Thompson/Getty Images.

Typeset in Sabon LT Std by SX Composing DTP, Rayleigh, Essex, SS6 9HQ
Printed and bound in Great Britain by Clays Ltd, Elcograf S.p.A.

Papers used by Piatkus are from well-managed forests
and other responsible sources.

Piatkus
An imprint of
Little, Brown Book Group
Carmelite House
50 Victoria Embankment
London EC4Y 0DZ

The authorised representative
in the EEA is
Hachette Ireland
8 Castlecourt Centre, Dublin 15,
D15 XTP3, Ireland
(email: info@hbgi.ie)

An Hachette UK Company
www.hachette.co.uk

www.littlebrown.co.uk

To Isabella

I hope that you can understand why Dad was away so often, and that you find the inspiration to do what you love with your life. Everything is possible with persistence and hard work. Always believe in yourself.

Contents

SOMEWHERE AROUND LAP 48 of the 2021 Abu Dhabi Grand Prix, I found myself sitting out the back of the garages of the Yas Marina F1 paddock. I was having a cigarette with friend and Red Bull Racing colleague Steve Forty, and feeling pretty dejected.

'I can't believe we've managed to blow it, Steve!'

I couldn't come to terms with the way the season had panned out. The whole team had been so strong and it looked at points like we were going to walk away with both the constructors' and drivers' championships. Now, after all the work, heartache and sacrifice, we were just minutes from walking away with nothing.

'You never know, mate, anything could still happen!' Steve replied in an attempt to stay positive.

If I'm honest, it didn't help and I'm not sure that even he believed it.

I'm not a quitter, though. I'll do anything within my power to win. And, when I walked back into the garage on lap 50 to see the screens showing Williams's Nicholas Latifi in the wall, I knew that an opportunity to change the course of sporting history might be about to present itself. Seeing the severity of the accident and realising that it would definitely result in the safety car being deployed, I knew what was coming next. The voice in my earpiece echoed what we were all thinking in the garage.

'Pitstop imminent, double stop imminent.'

This instruction from sporting director Jonathan Wheatley lit a fuse in the garage. Everybody exploded out of their seats and was up and ready in a flash. We knew that we were about to perform the most important pitstop of our lives.

'Fifteen seconds to a double stop; Verstappen first on the road.'

The signal triggered the crew of eighteen to file into the pitlane and ready ourselves for the arrival of the car. After thirteen years in the pitlane, I'm no stranger to adrenaline. In fact, I'm a bit of a junkie. The moments that came during that double stop are still a blur, but I know I was running on pure adrenaline. For the first time that year, there were no nerves, no thoughts. We had nothing to lose, and everything to gain. My body was acting almost autonomously. There was no need to focus on the wheel nut: my arms and hands just moved as they should do.

It was almost like those final pitstops were just something that happened rather than something that we did.

When I returned to the garage to see Max Verstappen rejoin the racetrack on new tyres, with only lapped cars between himself and leader Lewis Hamilton, I knew it was time for something extraordinary to happen.

Screams of 'Let's fucking go!' rang out around the garage as race control debated with team bosses as to how – or even whether – the race would resume with just three laps to go. Once those debates had played out and the two championship contenders rounded the corner to begin the final lap, there was a brief, tense silence. I've never before, and will likely never again, experienced an atmosphere like the one in the Red Bull Racing garage during that final lap of that 2021 season, when Max overtook Lewis.

As he crossed the line to become the 2021 Formula One world champion, I looked around at the tears of joy in some of my teammates' eyes and realised what it meant to all of us. It was everything. All of the pain of the last eight years, all of the work that had been done to get to this point, all of the stress and heartache . . . it had all paid off.

After the chequered flag had dropped and Max was crowned the champion, and as the commotion went on behind the scenes as teams' representatives battled over the final outcome of the race in the steward's office, I sat alone on the pit wall.

I was just soaking in the feeling of being a winner, mentally ticking the box of an achievement that had evaded me and my teammates for so long. As I watched my colleagues jump around the garage in ecstasy and consume beers at an alarming rate, one question kept floating around my mind while I sat looking down the now eerily quiet Abu Dhabi pitlane: 'How on earth did I end up here?'

Well . . . this is the story of how. This is my life in the pitlane.

This is a book to inspire change and progress within the world of motorsport. There are two reasons I wanted to write it. The first is that I wanted to open up the world of F1 like never before – to shine a light on the realities of life off the track: the good and the bad. I find myself harbouring a feeling of great responsibility towards those who might embark on this amazing journey after me, and want people to know both what they're in for, as well as how to get in there and experience it all in the first place. Having a real, authentic insight into the sport I now love would have been invaluable in helping me to start my career sooner, and to progress faster once I began. I consider myself extremely lucky to have been able to travel the world ten times over, building the fastest race cars on the planet as part of the world's most extreme circus. When I think about my life in Formula One, I know that, even long after I've put the spanners down, I won't ever quite be able to let it go. Such is the impact that the sport, the people and the lifestyle have had on me: my experiences will be ingrained for ever.

As well as providing this insight, I want to inspire those who traditionally might not choose to pursue careers in engineering. Over the last five years, the governing bodies, teams and owners throughout the industry have been asked to look at how they can make the sport more inclusive, with the aim of allowing the growing and diverse fanbase to feel better represented. As someone with first-hand experience of some of the barriers that people from underrepresented groups face when pursuing careers in racing, I've watched with great interest and involved myself in the process of making motorsport a more accessible industry.

When the sport opened its doors to Netflix and started to fully embrace the power of social media, I found myself in the spotlight more than I had ever bargained for. I was (and still am) inundated with messages from people all over the world, explaining that seeing me, a man of colour, succeed in a sport that was traditionally dominated by white European men had inspired them to pursue a career in racing. It was reading these messages that helped me to realise just how important representation is to people, and how the lack of representation from people who looked like me had affected my own confidence early in my career.

People had so many questions, and while teams were opening up and sharing insight into the drivers and the cars, there was still so little information about how one could go about pursuing a career in racing. I still try to answer as many people's messages as I can, but attempting to put the advice I have to offer in a message with a tiny character count is a thankless task. So, I sit here writing this book because I want anyone with an interest in engineering to know that, in motorsport, there is a job for you somewhere that will allow your natural talents to shine. If this book inspires just one person who wouldn't previously have considered a career in racing, then I will consider it a success.

While motorsport has seemingly become more accessible over the last ten years and the fanbase has grown dramatically, insight from those on the ground and working in the pitlane at every Grand Prix still isn't that easy to come by. I wanted to highlight the realities of choosing to spend nearly two hundred days of the year on the road. The highs, the lows and all of the stories that you won't hear on Netflix have amounted to an incredible career doing something that I love. I feel very privileged to have experienced it all myself, and I wanted to share it with those who also have a love for all things racing.

Sometimes, like Red Bull Racing at Yas Marina in 2021, all you need is a chance.

CHAPTER 1

The Starting Grid

The first questions people ask me when I tell them what I do for a living are inevitably, 'How did you get involved in racing?' or 'Did you know when you were young that it was what you wanted to do?'

In a career that requires such commitment and willingness to make significant sacrifices, people tend to assume that, much like the path a driver might take, engineers and technicians in motorsport all begin their journey at a young age. While I was typically that child who took everything apart, who wanted to know how everything worked and who would be more interested in how the magician did a trick than the illusion itself, I didn't know what I wanted to do with my life until long after I'd left school.

One of my only regrets throughout my career is simply not discovering racing earlier. I wish I'd been shown all of the amazing things that careers in motorsport can entail when I was fifteen, rather than discovering them in my twenties. The travel, the adrenaline, the pressure . . . I didn't know I loved all those things until I was already doing the job. Had I known earlier, I would have had the opportunity to steer my focus in the right direction years before I finally found what I loved doing.

For me, one of the greatest failings in the modern British education system is its inability – or lack of desire – to teach engineering in a practical environment. While, for many state-run British schools, engineering is too expensive to teach in a practical way, in my private north London school there simply wasn't much interest. The school was expected to produce doctors, lawyers and CEOs, not mechanics. I've always felt that the moment it became apparent to my teachers that I had no intention of being a lawyer or a doctor, or contributing to the school's proud heritage of sending students off to Oxford and Cambridge, I was no longer considered to be worth the bother.

I try not to sound ungrateful when I talk about my time at school. When I look back, I fully appreciate how fortunate I was to have had the education it provided me with, and I understand how hard my mother worked to ensure that she could give me a better education and chances in life than she had herself. She has been a constant driving force in my life. Persistent and resilient, her sheer determination to not allow me to fail was a huge influence on my later successes. She shaped my own determined and stubborn nature.

As an adult thinking now about providing the very best for my own daughter, I can appreciate why my mother was so determined to send me to a good school with a good reputation, whatever the cost. I have to say, though, at the time, I absolutely hated that school, and I got the impression the school hated me too.

Admittedly, I was a difficult student. It wasn't that I struggled with the difficulty of any of the work, it was that I struggled to stay interested and once I was distracted, or bored, I was then generally disruptive. This is still true of me today, to be perfectly honest. The school completely failed to notice that the subjects where I excelled were the ones that challenged me the most. Engaging teachers and interesting subject matter were the simple things I required. Throughout my education, I would shine at biology, physics and, of course, all sports, but by the time I was fifteen I'd lost pretty much all interest in school, and the teachers at University College School seemed to have lost all interest in me.

Outside of the classroom, the environment was stressful too. I had plenty of friends at school (being good at sport afforded me a sort of inherent popularity), but I never really felt like I belonged there so I used to beg my mum to just send me to the local state-run school instead. I'd spend one evening at a wealthy school friend's bar-mitzvah party in some swanky hotel in the West End, and the next back in Newham, east London, at my grandmother's, the house my mum had grown up in. The two worlds couldn't have been further apart. In addition, I was one of very few Black students so, like early in my racing career, I stood out, or at least I felt like I did.

So, while I had plenty of friends in school, I never felt I was part of the same world as them. Many of them knew that they would never have to worry about work or money. Most of them would follow in their parents' footsteps as high-paid professionals or inherit their businesses. At the very least, they all knew that they'd have the connections to earn a good living in whatever they wanted to do. That just wasn't the case for me. While my mother worked herself to the bone, and did incredibly well to get us out of a rat-infested flat above a kebab shop in East Ham and into a far better environment in north London, we were a working-class family and I was always acutely aware that many of my peers seemed to be playing to a different set of rules to me.

If I had known all those years ago that I would eventually fall in love with motor racing, be a part of the most dominant pitstop crew the sport has ever seen and go on to win world championships, I would most definitely have left school at sixteen after completing my GCSEs. The truth is, I only stayed on to take A levels because my mum had given me an ultimatum: stay on at school and complete the education that she had worked very hard to provide for me, or leave, get a job and start paying rent. It was a perfectly reasonable demand on her part and she knew that I had absolutely no intention of doing the latter. So, I stayed on, choosing to continue studying only the subjects that I knew I was already good at and therefore wouldn't challenge me too much. By this point, I'd mentally checked out of education anyway. I was far too busy chasing girls, clubbing and messing around with cars and motorbikes. But to appease my mother I took A levels in English, English literature and theatre studies. These qualifications obviously weren't chosen to prepare me for a career in motorsport, or with racing in mind at all, but I was good at them.

A lot of young people now message me on Instagram and ask what they should study if they want to be an F1 mechanic and I tend to say that, at fifteen or sixteen, the best advice I can offer is to study what you're good at and enjoy. The motorsport industry has grown so much over the last ten years that it now offers a much wider variety of careers than it did fifteen years ago. If you have a passion for racing, you can afford to take the time to discover what you're good at and then find a career that allows you to utilise those skills doing something that you love. Of course, I didn't know this when I was eighteen, and I just got lucky.

While I hadn't chosen those A levels with a STEM (science, technology, engineering and mathematics) career in mind, that's not to say that they haven't all come in handy at some point over the years. For starters, I'm writing this book about the job I love. In addition, I'm sure that some of the managers that have had to deal with me over the years have dreaded receiving well-written, succinct emails where I have eloquently, but ever so politely, explained why I am right and they are an idiot.

In fact, I'd now tout my written and verbal communication skills as some of the most valuable qualities that I can offer a race team. Undoubtedly, studying English and theatre studies A levels are both contributing factors to that. They also helped me to hone the 'soft skills' that are now considered an absolute must-have for somebody in a senior role in a modern Formula One team. For me, the ability to explain faults concisely and feed that information back to the design and engineering teams is crucial. Knowing how to provide succinct instructions, and produce documents that outline procedures that can be followed by anyone (and that will always result in the same outcome), allows me to hand over work to other technicians and train juniors to identical standards. So, while at the time I may not have chosen these subjects with motorsport in mind, the knowledge I gained led me to develop some of my most valuable skills.

Two years and three A levels later and I still had absolutely no idea what I wanted to do with my life, with the only certainty in my mind being that university wasn't going to be a path that I wanted to take. I'd simply had enough of being in a classroom and, as I had no idea what degree I'd even want to study for, I couldn't see the benefit of racking up a load of student debt for something that I'd likely never use.

At home, however, my mother's ultimatum still applied. I could go to university or I could get a job. So, I kicked about for a little while, working various jobs just to put a bit of money in my pocket. The list of those jobs is long and varied. It includes everything from retail to building-site labouring and forklift driving. For a short time, I worked in an Arla milk-bottling factory. The worst of them was definitely selling televisions in the electronics department of John Lewis. I've never enjoyed being inside all day or in windowless rooms. It's something that I struggle with now during the off-season. Driving to and from work in the dark during the winter months kills me.

Prior to racing, the best job I ever had was at Uptown Records in Soho, London – a small, independent record shop selling hip-hop, house and UK garage on vinyl. It was a job that my dad had managed to get me as it was owned and run by friends of his. My dad, in his younger years before he joined the fire service, was a DJ and his love of music is something that I've definitely inherited. I absolutely loved working in the record shop. Selling records and playing music all day didn't really feel like work at all. I have an incredible record collection as a result of my time at Uptown, but as vinyl became a thing of the past and sales in record shops dwindled, I knew I'd have to find something else to do with my life.

At the time, my only other interests were sport and cars. As much as I loved sport, my interest in playing had mostly faded once I left school. I had always been mechanically minded; as a child, I was desperate to figure out how every toy or appliance worked, rather than just what it did. As I got older, this naturally became a love of all things motorised. I passed my driving test about a week after my seventeenth birthday (my dad had been teaching me to drive for quite some time in the area around his office), and I'd become instantly involved in the modified car scene in north London, modifying my Honda Civic without telling my mum. I'd be out until the early hours most nights, among the street-racing scene in the industrial estates around Lakeside in Essex or back and forth to Southend at the weekend in a whole manner of modified motors with my friends. It was somewhere around this time that I decided I'd probably make a good mechanic, but I was still some way from turning that idea into a reality.

While I'd been hopping around London enjoying my newfound freedom from education at eighteen years old, a former school friend of mine, a guy named Daniel Speed, had been working as an apprentice at a very small north London garage during his gap year before he went off to university to study engineering. Before he left, he introduced me to the owner of Ridge Garage, Steve, who offered me the opportunity to take Dan's place once he had moved on. I accepted simply because it was the only decent offer out there to make some money and keep me out of trouble, and, conveniently, the garage was only ten minutes from home.

Now, you wouldn't think much of Ridge Garage if you drove past and looked at it from the outside. It looked a bit like someone's shed but with a sign outside. It was squashed in between a café (that has also been a Chinese, an Indian and a Turkish restaurant in my time) and someone's house. Steve was the kind of guy who could never turn down work. No job was too big and he'd take on absolutely anything. He'd built a very loyal customer base in the twenty or so years that he'd been there and, while other workshops came and went throughout the local area, Steve's clients would not take their cars anywhere else.

The environment at Ridge was perfect for me. It was a 'get stuck in and figure it out' kind of place, and there were very few rules other than to get the job done and keep Steve's customers happy. As another bonus, it was cash-in-hand weekly pay and, once I'd proven my ability after a few months, Steve paid me well for an eighteen-year-old with no mechanical qualifications.

I was also very lucky to have a couple of great mechanics to learn from. Steve wasn't a mechanic himself, but he employed two very good ones. Tomer, a young British-Israeli, was incredibly well-qualified and he'd been in the game for a while when we met. He was well-versed in the newer technologies that road cars were more frequently being equipped with, and he was fast – very fast.

I remember wondering why Tomer was working in such a small, independent garage, rather than enjoying all the perks and the shiny new workshop of a service centre for a main car dealer. I discovered that he had already worked at quite a few larger garages, but he said that he never enjoyed the rigmarole of doing the same work day-in, day-out. Plus, Tomer had a sweet deal at Ridge. He was earning good money as the most experienced mechanic and was in charge by default. Steve, not being a mechanic himself, couldn't really offer any oversight on what was going on, so Tomer pretty much did whatever he wanted and Steve was happy to just talk to customers and ring up the invoices. Tomer was also very confident in his own ability. Sometimes this came across as arrogance, and I think that this was probably at least partly to blame for his inability to get along with people in a larger workforce.

I realised almost immediately that he and I were quite similar in one particular aspect: we were both extremely competitive. Tomer would have been perfectly suited to the world of racing. After a few months, when I'd started to get up to speed, Tomer and I would often compete to see who could complete regular service work the quickest. While he obviously had the advantage of being far more experienced than I was, I would quite proudly manage to take the odd win.

Confident, competitive characters can become an incredibly efficient team under the right circumstances. Channelled correctly, that intra-team competition can drive you forward as a group. Certainly, on our best days, the cars would be flying through the garage, one after the other, as Tomer and I competed to get the most done. What I didn't realise at the time was that all of the little tricks and shortcuts that I was learning while racing Tomer to get a nice old lady's clutch changed would later be used to my advantage when I went racing.

My other new colleague at Ridge Garage was an older guy named Ken. First-generation British-Caribbean, Ken was brilliant and came with a wealth of experience of fixing absolutely anything. He must have been in his late fifties when I met him, and he had the car knowledge of a man who'd seen it all. In typically Caribbean style, Ken never rushed anything, much to the annoyance of Steve. He had no interest in competing with Tomer or rushing to get cars out the door, but whenever an old Saab arrived with a myriad of problems, Steve knew that Ken would be the man to fix it. I loved working with him as he never took himself too seriously and he always seemed to really enjoy teaching me.

He would often arrive at the garage in the morning, get a can of Coke from the off-licence across the street and then return to his toolbox, where he'd open a drawer and pull out a small bottle of Wray & Nephew overproof rum. He'd add this to his Coke and sip it throughout the day. In contrast to the races I'd have with Tomer, Ken would quite happily just sit and point at stuff and let me get on with it. He'd shout, 'Call me if you need me,' as he went outside for a cigarette in the alley down the side of the garage.

Things had been going well at Ridge, and within a year I had become a fairly proficient mechanic working on a whole manner of vehicles, earning decent money and enjoying it. Although I still didn't have much interest in organised racing, it was during this period at Ridge Garage that I started to realise that I wanted a career as a mechanic. I hadn't really taken any time to think about my long-term future or how I would achieve it. I just assumed things were going to work themselves out somehow.

Then, late in 2008, Steve pulled me aside to tell me that he was making me redundant. The financial crisis was hitting all businesses hard and the garage had been struggling. When Steve explained to me that he needed to let someone go and that as I had joined the most recently, it needed to be me, I was devastated. While I understood the reason, it's hard not to take redundancy personally. Especially when it's such a small business.

I felt like I was back to square one. Even worse, I now had some sense of what I wanted to do, but not the qualifications to go and do it. So, for a little while, I went back to the building site with my uncle Vere. I fell into a bit of a malaise, struggling for motivation and indecisive about how I was going to get back to working on cars. I looked at some college courses and thought about what path I could take as a mechanic from there. All of the options seemed to involve ending up working nine-to-five in a dealership, doing the same servicing work day-in, day-out, and filling out paperwork. While I knew that I could earn decent money like that, I also knew that it just wasn't what I wanted, but it would take me another few months before my desire to go out and find some new goals would be reignited.

One of the things that I now realise has always been important to me is that I never want to feel like a number. As a travelling technician in Formula One, where the team is limited to just sixty operational personnel, the work that you do at the track always has an appreciable value. Whether it's my responsibilities with regard to power unit assemblies or my performance in the pitlane, my work doesn't go unnoticed and that is more important to me than I realised when I was younger. At Ridge Garage, it was the same thing. Small businesses find it much easier to make employees feel appreciated compared to large multi-million-pound companies with thousands of employees.

Whenever I'm back in north London, I'll always pop in to Ridge Garage to catch up with Steve and see how things are going. What neither of us knew back in 2008 was that Steve probably did me the biggest favour anyone could have asked for when he let me go. Whenever he asks me how my career is going and I talk about racing, he'll say, 'I knew you'd be all right.'

I always shrug it off but the truth is, had Steve not made me redundant that day, I may well still be there, up to my elbows in grease doing the same jobs I was doing all those years ago. I can't imagine that I'd have ever discovered racing as a career had I continued working at Ridge, even for another year. After all, I was pretty happy, I had a boss whose only rule was to get the work done, I was getting paid in cash weekly and my commute was less than ten minutes. The garage also provided me with somewhere to work on my own cars out of hours, and Tomer and I spent most nights in the garage with music blaring, drinking beers and prepping cars to take to some illegal street-racing event the following weekend. As a nineteen-year-old with no real responsibilities and little ambition, it was blissful.

My mum, on the other hand, was probably happy that it had come to an end. There was no way she was going to have spent tens of thousands of pounds on a private education for me to end up coming home looking like I'd been down the mines, covered head to toe in dirt and grease. While she never said anything at the time, I know she was relieved when I finally got my shit together.

She took it upon herself to try to inspire me. After about six months of me being back to my previous post-school lack of ambition, my mum told me that a friend of hers, Margaret McDonagh, had invited her to the 2009 British Grand Prix at Silverstone and that there was a ticket for me if I wanted to come. I was hesitant at first, needing to be convinced to go and enjoy a day out in a hospitality suite.

When I think about that now, it seems absurd. I'd love a weekend in the paddock club for nothing! As always, my mum pushed me and, as always, she eventually got her way. I definitely should have been more thankful to her at the time, knowing now that, of the many seeds of opportunity she gave me over the years, this was the one that would take root.

There are only a few things that I remember about that day in Silverstone. Having spent so much time at that circuit over the last fifteen years, a lot of it has become a blur. I wasn't, at this point, really a motorsport fan and I'd never really paid much attention to Formula One. In fact, pretty much the only thing I did know about the sport was that Lewis Hamilton, a young mixed-heritage guy from Stevenage, had just become the world champion. My knowledge of the sport genuinely didn't extend much further.

I do have two crystal-clear memories of that day. The first is of sitting next to the UK soul singer Lemar (who was a pretty big deal at the time) in the VIP hospitality seating. We laughed that neither of us had a clue what was going on during the race, and I remember us trying to work out who was winning.

The other memory, and this is seared into my brain as clear as the day it happened, is of the pitlane walk prior to the race. It was a light-bulb moment for me. This thirty-minute experience walking up and down the pitlane in a hideous brown Adidas tracksuit, watching the teams prepare their cars and do pitstop practice prior to the start of the Grand Prix, made me say to my mum, 'I could do that job.'

I watched the mechanics carry out their routine race preparation and I realised that most of the jobs they were doing were not really that much different from the work that I had done at Ridge Garage. The moment at which my interest was well and truly sparked was when I saw one of the teams begin their pre-race pitstop practice. It was at some point during this, as I leaned over the barriers to get the best view possible, that my mind went from thinking 'I could do that' to 'I'm *going* to do that'.

Back in 2009, there was very little information around about how to begin a career in motorsport. Only a few colleges offered motorsport-specific engineering courses and they were largely theory-based learning. The only place you'd ever see what kind of jobs were available at race teams was in the back of *Autosport* magazine each week. After paying a visit to Bedford autodrome to meet a friend of a friend who was then working in F2, I learned that the National College for Motorsport was based at Silverstone Circuit. I still had pretty much no clue how I was going to carve out a career in racing, so I took the advice of this friend and sought to enrol.

Looking at the campus and reading the prospectus, I thought I was unlikely to get accepted. The college was really small at the time, only taking about sixty students a year. By this point, I was nearing twenty and the college usually took students aged seventeen or so after they'd completed their GCSEs. I booked myself on to an open evening and toured the workshops, looking at the various cars that students got to work on and take to the track and run open test sessions with, learning how to run a race car. The facility was impressive; there was a wide variety of different junior formula cars, a couple of Ginettas, and plenty more.

The thing that caught my eye almost immediately was a Formula One front wing, sitting atop one of the workbenches in the corner of the main workshop. It was a white 'Earth Dreams'-liveried wing from the BAR Honda car that had never seen the circuit as Honda had pulled out of the sport before the start of the season. It was a beautiful piece of engineering.

I spoke to the head of the college and all of the tutors on the open evening, and pretty much begged them to give me a place at the college. They had a lot of applicants for those sixty spaces, and they had concerns that I would be the oldest student that they'd ever had. I assured them that I'd also be the best student they'd ever had. I was confident in my ability as a mechanic and it probably showed. Unlike many of the other applicants, I wasn't a kid any more.

When the college wrote to offer me a place, I told myself that this was the beginning of my journey, the first step towards finding a career that I might actually enjoy. Up until this point, most of my friends would have quite rightly described me as unambitious or even indifferent in terms of my future. That was true, to an extent. I'd just never found anything that I saw as both enjoyable long term as a career and a realistic prospect for what I could do well with my skillset. With my enrolment at the National College for Motorsport, that was about to change.

CHAPTER 2

Learning Opportunity

My understanding of the importance of where I was in life in comparison to my peers at the National College for Motorsport (partly due to the difference in age between us) gave me a distinct advantage in terms of the prospects of me securing my first motorsport job. I was a more experienced mechanic with an understanding of the basics already, and I was past that point where most young men really aren't that focused at all – I knew what I wanted. I figured that I'd be a much more attractive candidate for apprenticeships compared with those younger than me, as they were learning a trade straight from school and, in some cases, learning it from scratch. While I recognised this advantage almost immediately (it became fairly apparent within just a couple of hours) this was also the first time, probably since I'd played sport at school, that my fiercely competitive nature started to shine through. Competing with Tomer had just been a bit of fun – now, I was competing for my future.

I should probably stress at this point that I am, and always have been, a sore loser. Now, while on paper that may not seem the wisest of qualities to embrace in life, in motorsport it's often a trait that suits perfectly. A naturally competitive personality is commonplace in any race team, and mine undoubtedly comes from my mother. For the most part, race mechanics aren't just there to collect a wage – there are far simpler and less stressful ways for a mechanic to earn money – no, we're here to win. I've always felt that nobody is entitled to win and, in this game, you eat what you kill. You are only going to grind out the result if you're willing to do more, learn faster, work harder and think smarter, and you may still need a bit of luck here and there . . . sounds just like motor racing to me!

So, it was clear to me that being outperformed by any of the other students wasn't an option. I say this not to sound disrespectful to them, but to demonstrate that I felt as though, with the position I was in, failure to be at the top wouldn't be an easy pill to swallow.

While being a more mature student had its advantages, I had no pedigree in motorsport or engineering at all. A lot of the other students, in fact most them, either had close family or friends involved in racing or lived in the rural areas in the UK where motorsport takes place. They had been involved in the sport already, or had at least been exposed to it.

I knew cars, I knew how they worked, but I was a kid from the city who, until a couple of months earlier, hadn't been within a hundred feet of a real race car. My mechanical knowledge was limited to cars that I'd worked on in a small garage in north London. And we're only talking about servicing work on your average, everyday road cars. (I'll never forget – or miss – the 'joys' of working on some old, rusty, 200,000-mile minicab.) My technical knowledge of race cars was, at best, vague, so I had plenty to learn about them and, actually, I still do. Having spent the last ten years working on only one particular car every year, each one a development of the last, there are still so many motorsport disciplines that I'd love to learn more about. Now, with a skillset that's largely universal in the industry, I'd love to do a World Rally Championship or a Dakar Rally, should the opportunity present itself. I'd certainly consider taking on another Le Mans.

So, the plan for college was simple: I needed an NVQ2 and 3 in Performing Engineering Operations and a BTEC qualification as a Race Technician. In terms of the actual course material, it didn't feel like it was going to challenge me too much. It turned out that the basic workings of junior series race cars, the type I'd be learning on at college, were far simpler than those of the cars that I'd been working on daily at Ridge Garage. The mechanical engineering of these cars is fairly simple by design. Brakes, steering assemblies and fluid systems on road cars are far more complex and difficult to service and repair than on a small Formula Ford car, for example. Once you've successfully changed the timing chains on a 3.0l Audi diesel, you'll be ready for anything.

To be honest, I didn't really enrol at the college just for the certificates. I was there for the opportunities. The National College for Motorsport was where junior formula motorsport teams in and around the UK came looking for students to potentially take on as apprentices. I was in a hurry, too; being in an environment with kids that were a couple of years younger than me made me feel like I was lagging behind. I needed to get on with it, 'get this apprenticeship, get into the workplace'. Bear in mind that I'd gone from earning decent money, cash in hand, to now being back at college three days a week and picking up odd jobs on the other days. I was on the lookout for that first racing opportunity. Fast.

My lead tutor, Justin Downard, was not only a great educator but also an experienced race technician. It was clear to me that, having had a career that included travelling roles with the Lotus F1 team and British touring cars, and that spanned a couple of decades, this was some-one who would have all the knowledge that I needed to start my own journey. Because of the relationship he had with motorsport teams up and down the country, one of the roles that he took on for the college was connecting students with teams that could potentially be their future employers.

Over the course of the last fifteen years, I've received many pieces of advice or instruction on how I might advance my career. Whenever people ask me what the path to F1 is for a race technician, or ask me what they need to do, I remind them that there is no one definitive pathway, there are many. One of the very first pieces of advice Justin gave us is the same as I now give to anyone who asks me how they might begin the pursuit of a career in motorsport: you have to start building a network, and see where that takes you. In order to do that, you first need to find some racing near you – any racing. Karting, drag racing, rallying, drifting, even a lawnmower-racing club. That might sound a little ridiculous, but this is about much more than turning spanners. On almost any given weekend, a racing venue close enough for you to access will be hosting a motorsport event of some sort and, in the days leading up to that event, you can usually pay a small fee (or, in a few cases, nothing at all) to walk down the paddock and see teams preparing all manner of different vehicles. Walking through a paddock and talking to those working in the garages is an opportunity to engage with somebody who might be able to provide you with that first bit of work experience that you will need as you start to build a CV.

When most people think of motor racing, their first thought (certainly in the UK) is Formula One. It's understandable. Obviously, F1 has always been considered by most as the technological and engineering pinnacle of motorsport. But what a lot of budding engineers and technicians don't realise, and I certainly didn't, is just how large and far reaching the 'pyramid' is that leads to this pinnacle. There are some great resources available now (which I will detail later) that can help you find these organisations and events. This motorsport pyramid is vast and made up of thousands of small privateer teams all the way up to the large, successful outfits of the World Endurance Championship (WEC), MotoGP and F1, all competing at different levels, in different disciplines and with, of course, different budgets. You need to find these smaller teams – at their workshops, at races or at other events – and go to see them. Whether it's an open-track testing day, a national junior formula race weekend or a karting race, you need to approach these teams, state your intent, and volunteer to help in any shape or form they're willing to allow.

If you were to imagine the first layer of bricks in a pyramid, in terms of motorsport series you would find junior karting, local club racing such as the events run by the British Racing and Sports Car Club (BRSCC) or British Automobile Racing Club (BARC), with categories in various disciplines, and the historic racing that happens at the likes of Goodwood Revival and Silverstone Festival (previously known as Silverstone Classic). Moving up, you'll find important junior categories such as the GB3 Championship (the current name for the British Formula Three championship), where drivers such as Ayrton Senna, Mika Häkkinen and Emerson Fittipaldi made names for themselves. Further towards the summit, series such as the British and World Touring Car Championships lead the way to the prestigious German touring car series DTM (originally called the Deutsche Tourenwagen Masters) as well as the hotly contested British Rally Championship. As you reach the pinnacle of motorsport in Europe, you'll be looking at series such as WEC, MotoGP and, of course, Formula One.

Just like you wouldn't expect to go and cook in a Michelin-star restaurant straight after taking your first community cooking class, almost nobody in the F1 pitlane started their careers there. The common theme among the mechanics and technicians I work with in the F1 paddock is that very few, if any, have a degree-level qualification in engineering. While all of our trackside engineers and strategists do indeed have engineering degrees, those of us who build the cars, service and maintain them over the course of the race weekend and perform pitstops on Sunday bring something far more valuable to the work we do. That crucial thing is a wealth of experience and understanding of the assemblies for which we are responsible.

In his book *Outliers*, the writer and thinker Malcolm Gladwell famously wrote about needing to put in more than 10,000 hours of work to become an expert, and F1 is no different. Those 10,000 hours (though in reality it's far more) of practical experience are what you need to be considered for a travelling role in an F1 team. If you dream of being a motorsport mechanic or technician, your experience and the references that come with that experience will be worth more to you than your qualifications. When you find that first smaller team that says 'Yeah, OK,' and allows you to come and assist them while learning over the course of a race event, your reward for that work will be your first bit of experience, and hopefully a good reference . . . and now, you build.

Another thing that's absolutely essential is something that I didn't even realise I needed until after it had happened. Quite simply, you need to fall in love with the sport. There is one basic thing that I share with everybody that I work with now: we all love racing, in its purest and most basic sense. Regardless of how talented you might be or how hard you're willing to work, if you don't absolutely love racing then my suggestion is that you do something else for more money.

So now I'm twenty years old, I've set my first long-term career goal and I've got the first piece of advice on how I need to begin. I just needed to get on with it.

One of the benefits of being a student at the National College for Motorsport was that its location, in the grounds of Silverstone Circuit, allowed for unique opportunities to seek employment from the numerous small teams and businesses also based there. On top of that, it also provided access to the paddock itself, most of the time, and first-hand knowledge of what events were going on throughout the year. Anyone who lives or works around the track or in Whittlebury village, just the other side of the circuit, will know that there's always some sort of event going on. I'm sure that many of the racing fans in the village could probably identify from the noise which type of vehicles were on the track on any particular day.

Our college passes would allow us access to the circuit most of time and I used to take the opportunity to walk into the circuit and around the paddock on most days during my lunch. This was where my first opportunity to gain some real experience of being a race technician presented itself.

A couple of months into my time at the college, Justin mentioned one Monday morning that the annual Britcar 24HR was taking place at Silverstone Circuit the following weekend. I didn't know much about Britcar other than it being 'tin-top racing'. Tin-top refers to closed-top chassis, touring cars, GT racing and the like. The vehicles were not too dissimilar to the road cars I was used to servicing back at Ridge Garage, but very different from the monocoque 'formula' cars that I later chose to work on. It's worth noting that once you strip a road car of its comforts, conveniences and ancillary systems, and only leave what is required for it to function, you end up with pretty much what you can expect to see in a rudimentary race car. In fact, if you did this to your average Honda Civic, welded a tubular steel roll cage on to it, and made some safety modifications to the fuel system, you'd pretty much be at the point where you could enter it into a Britcar race. I'm sure some of you will remember an old episode of *Top Gear* where Jeremy Clarkson and co. entered a BMW into a race event. The event they entered was Britcar 24HR.

I didn't at this point know what type of racing was going to be the path I ended up taking. After all, I was still learning all of the different disciplines that made up the pyramid of motorsport. I didn't actually decide that F1 was my ultimate goal until a fair while later. I think that it was always going to end up that way, as I'm very much of the view that if I'm going to do anything, I have to aim to be the best at it, but I didn't have the confidence or understanding of the sport at the time to set myself that goal. While I was still just a college student, I knew enough about the industry already to see that breaking into Formula One wouldn't be easy. When I'd spent that brief time watching the mechanics in the pitlane prior to the British Grand Prix, it was clear to me that these people were the best at what they did. I wanted to learn so that, one day, I could say that about myself.

On the Wednesday before the Britcar 24HR race, I planned to use my lunch break to walk into the paddock and see if any of the teams running cars would allow me to join them for the weekend. I soon had to change my plans, though. I made an error in discussing this idea with another student, a friend of mine. The problem arose when he then discussed this with someone else, and the next thing I knew, almost every student at the college was planning to do the same thing. I remember how annoyed I was at myself for simply not keeping my plans to myself, something I'd later learn to be a valuable skill when working towards a career in racing.

I knew that only a limited number of teams were likely to be interested in taking on a college student for work experience, and I didn't want to give anyone else the opportunity to get down there first and beat me to it. So, I hatched a new plan . . . I went to my first class that morning, but had no intention of going to my second. In the walk between the classroom and the workshop, I peeled off to the car park. When I was asked where I was going, I simply responded that I'd 'forgotten something in the car' and that I'd catch up. I had absolutely no intention of going to our workshop session. By bunking off, something that I was perfectly familiar with from my time at school, I had bought myself at least two hours in the Silverstone paddock to approach teams before any other college students showed up asking for the same thing.

As anyone who follows Formula One will know, teams and individual personnel will do absolutely anything that they can get away with to gain a competitive advantage, even it is slightly beyond the limitations of the rules. Although I obviously knew that I shouldn't be skipping class, I also knew how supportive the college tutors were of our efforts to seek work experience, and that when I apologised and explained why I had done it, I was likely to be forgiven without any major issue. In stark contrast to my time at school, I got the impression that I was well liked by the teaching staff at the National College for Motorsport. To be fair, at this point in my life, I was far easier to manage as a student. I was driven, focused and mature in comparison to others. Being the oldest student that they had ever taken at the college, I was probably a breath of fresh air.

So, straight over to the paddock I walked. The event was being run from the old paddock and garages at Silverstone, the same ones that I had walked past when I'd attended the Grand Prix. It was noticeably quieter than it had been on that Sunday afternoon. This was before the Wing, the paddock that Formula One now uses, had been built, and the start/finish straight was moved to its current location in 2011.

I walked around for a while, watching teams both big and small unpack trucks, set up equipment in the garage and start to prepare for their weekend. I marvelled at some of the race cars and was surprised at the variety of the vehicles in the different classes, but all in the same race. If you're not familiar with Britcar, have a look at the entry lists over the years – it's quite an eye-opener. I can't think of another series where you'll find diesel-powered VW Golfs on the same track as V8-powered Moslers, Porsches and everything in between.

Walking around the paddock, basically begging to be allowed to come and work for free, was the first time in as long as I could remember that I'd felt in any way nervous or vulnerable. Although Justin had told us to prepare for plenty of people to turn us down before we found an opportunity, I knew that failure to get what I wanted would really piss me off because, for the first time in a long time, I really cared about what I was trying to achieve!

It must have been a good twenty minutes or so before I even plucked up the courage to ask a single team if there was any chance that they'd take me on for the weekend. That first team I approached had absolutely no intention of letting me anywhere near their garage; neither did any of the next ten teams I spoke to. It was a good lesson, even if all I learned was that the worst people can do is say, 'No.'

As I made my way down the paddock, I was conscious that with every 'No, sorry' or 'We don't take apprentices' that came my way, I was getting closer and closer to the very last garage. I was starting to accept that I may as well chalk up the whole plan as a loss and that I'd have to go back to college, apologise for my absence, and also explain that I'd failed. Then, with only a couple of teams left in the paddock to plead with, I struck gold.

A small father-and-son team, Aryliam Motorsport, owned by Clive Denham and running a Honda Integra DC4, said they would happily have me for the weekend, feed and water me, and teach me the basics. Most importantly of all, I knew that if I did a decent job, Clive would provide just the kind of reference I needed for my CV when trying to find a full-time apprenticeship at the end of my first year in college. This was it: I was going racing.

Walking back over to the college and crossing paths with groups of students just starting their lunchbreak and heading over to attempt what I had already achieved, I must say I felt pretty smug.

I found out later that one of the other students had seen me out of the window, walking away from the campus, and duly informed one of the college tutors what I was up to. So as soon as I arrived back, I sought out Michael Herbert, who was running the workshop, to apologise and explain. Herb was a great teacher, and a lovely person to match, so as soon as I told him that I'd been successful and that I'd be working at Britcar at the weekend, he commended me for my effort and forethought. Other than telling me to make sure I caught up with the notes, he had absolutely no issue with me missing the class. Perhaps he was even impressed by my initiative. Asking for forgiveness rather than permission had worked in this instance and, later on in my career, this philosophy would become my general policy.

It turned out that a few of my peers had also been successful in securing work over the Britcar weekend, two of them with teams that I had spoken to previously and that had told me categorically that they 'didn't take work experience or college students at all, sorry'. It wasn't lost on me that the only difference between me and the kids that had enquired about an hour after me was the colour of our skin. Ultimately, I didn't care. I had achieved the goal of my trip, my persistence had paid off, and if that was the reason, then dwelling on it wasn't going to help me move forward. I'd like to hope that actually all that had happened was that my enquiry had planted a seed in their minds and that they'd seen the benefit of having a volunteer by the time another student had come to enquire. After all, it was a good deal for the team. They'd just gained an extra set of hands for the next three days, for free.

Looking back at it now, this was probably the first time I'd ever had to consider whether my ethnicity would be a problem, or at least a barrier, to my success in motorsport. Up until this point, I'd not even had a thought about it, despite me being one of only two Black students in an intake of sixty or so. It was also the moment that I realised that my education, talent and confident nature couldn't protect me from this kind of implicit bias.

I couldn't have been more excited for the weekend. That event at Silverstone cemented my determination to continue to pursue a career in the pitlane. It was definitely the moment when I fell in love with racing. If you can spend all night running around in the pissing rain, cold, wet and working for free and still have a huge smile on your face for a week afterwards, then the chances are this is something that could be for you!

The experience of being in a paddock, working through the night in a twenty-four-hour race, was confirmation that I was on a path to a career doing something that I was going to love. I slept in my car from Friday night onwards in the paddock car park and, in typically British style, it really was a cold and wet weekend. Having gone back to being a student, I didn't really have a lot of money and, due to it being a race weekend, the bed and breakfast that I normally stayed in during the week for college was fully booked. So, despite my mother's kind offer to pay for a place for me to stay, I decided it was just easier to sleep in the car park of Silverstone Circuit in my Mk3 VW Golf – a compact car, to say the least! This was something that I did fairly regularly during my time at college. Motorsport, certainly early on in your career, is unlikely to be very glamorous. Sorry to disappoint you.

Earlier in the week, I did feel a little jealous of my peers who had managed to get in with the bigger outfits, running the V8 Moslers and the like, but being with a small, family-run team turned out to be a blessing in disguise. I found out later that those guys had done very little mechanical work at all. I guess the bigger teams had just figured out that they could get a bit of free labour and had no intention of actually doing any teaching. The guys told me that they'd pretty much just swept floors, emptied bins and cleaned wheels all weekend.

While I did spend a very cold and wet evening running tyres back and forth to the Dunlop tent in between pitstops, I'd managed to put enough of my knowledge on display for Clive to have me changing wheels and brakes, and doing all manner of other jobs throughout the practice and qualifying sessions. I even ended up refuelling the car during pitstops in the race.

I couldn't believe I was really building a race car in the garages at Silverstone Circuit only months after enrolling at college. This was the same pitlane that I had visited not long ago during the F1 Grand Prix weekend and been in awe watching the F1 mechanics do pitstop practice on Sunday morning prior to the race. Looking at the spare engine for the Honda Integra, boxed up in the corner of the garage, I couldn't help but wonder how quickly it could be changed during the race, should we have a failure. Unsurprisingly, the trusty Honda made it to the line with very few issues at all and, post-race, the spare engine was wheeled back onto the truck untouched.

I was in my element! It may only have been a weekend running tyres around for no pay at the bottom of that motorsport pyramid we'd had explained to us at college, but I had spent the weekend as a race mechanic for the first time. Clive and the team took me out to a local Indian restaurant to say thank you at the end of the weekend, and he put a few quid in my pocket while assuring me that he'd provide a glowing recommendation should I wish to use him as a reference going forward. Mission accomplished.

I often look at the pictures I took that weekend, and the ones I took in the Silverstone F1 pitlane in 2009. From time to time, if I'm feeling a little down or lacking motivation, I look at those photos to remind myself just how far I've come and to remember that, when I took them, I had absolutely no idea what the future would hold.

When I returned to college the following week, I felt a renewed drive and focus while strangely being much more relaxed. Perhaps having completed my first race event and having enjoyed it so much, any nerves or anxiousness about the career path I'd chosen had begun to fade. I knew I'd made the right decision and I felt that, if I was willing to work harder than those around me, I probably had a fair chance at success.

I told Justin on the Monday morning about my experience at Britcar – what a great time I'd had and what I'd learned – and he said that I looked knackered (I was) and that I could have just taken the day off and called in to explain. While that was true and I most certainly wasn't my best self on that Monday at college, I was ahead on most of my work and the course material wasn't particularly challenging anyway, so I could coast. On top of that, my attendance, even if I was a little worse for wear, made me look better than the guys who'd worked the weekend and then taken Monday off.

You see, when it came to apprenticeships, Justin, Herb and the other teaching staff had decisions to make. From their point of view, every time they sent a student out to a team that had come looking for apprentices, there was the opportunity for that student to cast the college in either a good or a less favourable light. If Justin was constantly sending teams apprentices that just couldn't cut it, were lazy or lacked the fundamental knowledge required, how long would it be before the teams stopped asking him? Just as I was saying earlier, reputation and references are everything in this game, and Justin had to protect not just his own but that of the college.

I wanted all of the tutors to know that I was the number-one prospect in our class of sixty; that if any of us was going to succeed long term, it was going to be me. So, I put in the work, I aced every assignment, showed up early, stayed late, took myself seriously and learned. One thing you can never do if you want to succeed early on is shy away from the work. Regardless of how technically skilled someone might be, race teams do not have time for people that can't use their initiative or put the extra effort in. This applies throughout motorsport, but that need to have the perfect people in every role is even more prevalent in modern-day Formula One. The cost cap that F1 teams now operate under leaves absolutely no room for personnel that aren't up to speed. There is no budget surplus and the job market is fiercer than ever.

I'd noticed that Justin had slowly been sending students out to race teams for work experience when they came looking and he hadn't thrown any of those chances my way, so I went to talk to him as I was concerned that perhaps there was something I wasn't doing well enough to be put forward. He tried to reassure me that he was simply waiting for 'something that was right for me' but with no further understanding of what that meant, this didn't sit well with me. Patience has never been a strong suit of mine: if I'm ready to go, I expect those around me to be the same. In this respect, it's a good job that I ended up where I am today, in a team where very few have patience and that's what helps us to get things done! Justin just about managed to put my mind at ease, and I got my head back down and into the syllabus and my assignments while he continued to look for the sort of opportunity that he had in mind for me. But I have to admit that I was frustrated.

When I look back at the college and how many students from that year have actually gone on to have successful, long-term motorsport careers, it becomes clear just how challenging an industry motorsport can be. Of the sixty or so students, a couple have just joined me in the F1 paddock, a few are doing junior formula racing in F2, some have had successful careers in WEC and one built himself a great life in Australia doing V8 supercars before deciding he'd simply had enough of racing. On the whole, I'd say maybe around ten or twelve of the sixty ended up actually pursuing racing careers successfully. In all honesty, if you'd asked me to predict how many it would be at the time, I would've expected the number to be lower. It's not an easy job and the further you progress, the more ruthless it gets.

One of my favourite memories from college was something that actually happened on our very first day. Jim Harrod, who was the head of the college, sat us all down that morning to talk about what we were about to embark on. He explained the syllabus and how it broke down into the different units, and he explained what kind of careers we'd be pursuing and how to get the most out of the resources available. He then remarked jokingly that we were at a college for mechanics and technicians, and that if we'd enrolled because we wanted to be racing drivers, we were definitely in the wrong place. It was at this point that a kid in the middle of the room immediately stood up, picked up his bag, and left. We never saw him again.

The list of anecdotes from my time at the National College for Motorsport is seemingly endless and I often reminisce with other former students when I bump into them in paddocks around the world. I once watched a student put an 8-mm thread tap into a pillar drill at high speed, while simply holding the piece of aluminium that he wanted to tap a thread into in his hand. Thankfully Herb shouted and stopped him before anybody was seriously injured. When asked what he was doing and why was he using the drill to tap the thread, the student simply replied that it would be quicker than doing it by hand. I don't think he was allowed to use any power tools for a long while after that.

One of the requirements for enrolment at the college was having maths and English GCSEs with at least a C grade. I can only imagine they had made some exceptions, because a week in to our workshop sessions it became apparent that one student had absolutely no idea how to read millimetres on a rule. He understood the concept of the metric system, so on paper he had no problem doing calculations, he'd just never actually measured anything. It seemed absurd to me at the time but what I realise now is how many schools in the UK struggle to teach STEM in a hands-on environment. Like so many of those I work with now, I am a kinaesthetic learner: I have to do things with my hands to fully understand them and this is why a trade college was such a perfect environment for me. It's a great first step for anyone wanting to work in a technical role in motorsport who doesn't feel the degree route is right for them.

CHAPTER 3

A Rise in Status

Justin came to see me at college one morning to tell me that one of the teams that he'd been hoping to introduce me to had contacted him, looking for an apprentice. His relationship with them was very good and the college had two former students working for them already. Justin asked me if I'd be able to drive back up to Silverstone on Thursday morning to meet with the chief mechanic at Status Grand Prix Racing.

Status was a small race team, running three single-seater cars competing in what was then called GP3 (now known as FIA Formula Three – the FIA is the Fédération Internationale de l'Automobile, the governing body for most motorsports, including Formula One). The team had initially been founded in 2005 to run 'Team Ireland' in the

A1 GP series – where drivers represented a country rather than a private team – before the series itself had run into legal and financial trouble and folded in 2009. Status was a business of only about twelve employees but, although it was small, it was still a well-funded and professional outfit that attracted talented up-and-coming drivers looking to make their way to Formula One.

I told Justin that I would of course go and meet with their chief mechanic on Thursday, but as it was only Tuesday, my impatience immediately kicked in. As Status GP's factory was only down the road on New Rookery Farm in Silverstone, I decided instead to pop in there that afternoon when I finished college.

When I tell people about taking the initiative in pursuit of work in motorsport, this is exactly the kind of thing I'm talking about. When small teams with small budgets are hiring, the person who chooses to deliver their CV by hand and introduce themselves has almost always put themselves in a better position to get an interview as opposed to the hundreds of people who have just sent their CVs by post or email. Certainly, when you get to the point of applying for F1 jobs and other larger teams, you need to follow whatever application process that they have put in place, but when you are trying to get that first appointment at the junior level, my advice will always be to try and make a personal connection with the hiring team. Going to open test days and walking around paddocks is a great way to do that. It helps to stop you being anonymous in a competitive industry.

I arrived at Status Grand Prix later that afternoon, as soon as I'd finished my college day. I walked into its quiet office and introduced myself. I was nervous, but knowing that Justin had told them to expect me, and also that my college uniform would help identify me and the reason why I'd come, helped to some degree. It was quite daunting, walking into a very quiet race-team office for the first time. There's that horrible feeling when you walk in and everyone who's sitting at their desks looks up at you simultaneously. Even fifteen years later, I hate walking into the Red Bull Racing design office for this exact same reason. It's like walking into a library and if you're an outsider, you immediately draw everyone's attention.

As I introduced myself to the room, a large, bearded man with a gold hoop earring and thick Bristolian accent stood up from his desk to shake my hand, welcome me and thank me for coming in. This was chief mechanic Paul Bellringer. I didn't know it at the time, but this handshake would be the beginning of one of my relationships in the sport for which I'm most grateful. This man would become one of my most respected mentors.

Paul was a fearsome-looking and larger-than-life character who was widely known as 'The Angry Pirate'. It's a misnomer as far as I can tell, as are so many nicknames I've encountered throughout my career. Paul would turn out be one of the calmest and most calming people I'd ever work with. Even when the shit truly hit the fan, I never saw Paul panic or break from his serene persona. I'll never forget that first meeting with Paul and how he managed to make me feel at ease almost immediately as he showed me around the Status workshop and introduced me to the other mechanics.

I want you to know that if you're on a path to a motorsport career, you will come across some amazing people in this industry, but very few who will have a vested interest in helping you on your journey. The competitive nature of people attracted to motorsport jobs (and in my experience mechanics as a whole), coupled with the scarcity of jobs as you climb the ladder to F1, mean that sometimes it can feel like it's not a team sport at all. It can very often feel like everyone is just out for themselves.

Paul turned out to be one of the biggest influences in my career and I couldn't have asked for a better role model at the very beginning of it. He was a tough, no-nonsense and straight-talking guy who, despite these attributes, always managed to make you feel loved. If you fucked up, he'd tell you about it, but he always emphasised that your failures were lessons and that they were going to happen at some point. The thing to ensure is that you never make the same mistake twice. There are a number of things that I still do today, and think about while I'm working, that were taught to me by Paul.

What is even more amazing is the number of mechanics I work with currently who were also influenced by Paul early in their careers. Currently at Red Bull Racing there are four or five mechanics that have worked directly for Paul Bellringer or know him from one project or another, and throughout the F1 paddock there are hundreds of people who have encountered him in some way throughout their careers. What is most incredible is that I'm yet to find anyone who has anything but respect for him. This is an almost impossible feat when you've had a motorsport career spanning three decades at the highest level. Paul had been the test team chief mechanic at BAR Honda during a time when there was no restriction on the amount of testing teams could do; it was by all accounts a brutal job. His wealth of knowledge was seemingly endless and even long after I'd moved on from Status GP, I would often ask Paul for advice and keep him updated as to how I was getting along.

The Status GP workshop was a nice facility and, as I was shown around it, my eyes were instantly drawn to the three fully built GP3 race cars sitting by the door waiting to be loaded onto a truck. GP3 was a feeder series for Formula One, and was later renamed FIA F3 to bring some uniformity to the drivers' ladder to F1; GP2 was later renamed FIA F2. The reason that Justin had been waiting for this opportunity to become available (rather than just sending me out to the first team that came calling) was that GP3 was a pretty big deal for a first proper motorsport job. The GP3 calendar, as the F3 calendar does now, followed all of the European rounds of Formula One, so naturally it meant that on race weekends you'd be sharing the pitlane with F1 teams in between the F1 sessions.

Status was also a very good outfit. They were well managed, had plenty of budget and the drivers were good. Future Red Bull junior driver and Formula E champion António Félix da Costa partnered the incredibly talented *Autosport* Award-winning Alexander Sims in 2011, my first full season at the team.

I spent the next few weeks popping into Status at the end of my college day, helping out where I could, making the mechanics cups of tea, cleaning and doing anything else I could to prove that I was serious and wanted a job. After a while, Paul officially offered me the apprentice position and I couldn't have been happier. While it was just a start, more than anything at this point I really needed to get back to earning a wage. This apprenticeship also meant that I no longer had to attend college three days a week: I could simply finish and submit my coursework in my own time and instead do the rest of my learning on the job, which was perfect for me. I was determined to show Justin Downard that the faith he had placed in me was warranted, and I assured him that I wouldn't let him down.

My appointment at Status also meant that, for the first time, I would get to do pitstops on a formula-spec car. Pitstops in F2 and F3 are quite different from Formula One in terms of how they are performed. In Formula One, a pit crew features eighteen people: three people per corner to change the wheels, two to operate the front and rear jacks lifting the car as it arrives in the box, two people to adjust either side of the front wing and two people either side of the car to steady it while the wheels are being changed. You need that number of people to have the car stop and go in around two seconds. The pitlane personnel limit for F2 and F3 means that it isn't possible for stops to be performed the same way. It means that on each corner, only one person is responsible for undoing the wheel nut, removing the wheel, fitting the new one and retightening the nut.

In GP3, there were no regularly scheduled pitstops during a race as the distance covered didn't necessitate a change of tyres. The only times you would need to pit in a GP3 race were if the weather changed and you needed to fit wet tyres or if the car had been involved in an incident that required a new front wing or tyres due to a puncture.

Regardless, pitstop practice became part of the routine throughout the week, and I was hooked immediately. In fact, I was addicted to pitstops. I wanted to practise much more frequently, so one of the No. 1 mechanics and I asked Paul to have a static rig made for the factory so people could practise during any downtime, should they wish. Paul agreed, much to the disappointment of the appropriately named 'Grumps', our truckie (which in motorsport tends to mean someone who helps to look after equipment as well as driving and maintaining the trucks). He would constantly have to be recharging compressed air bottles after they'd been emptied, by me, throughout the day, every single day. There was also a rapidly growing pile of destroyed aluminium wheel nuts. That's what practice is for, and I made sure that I got plenty of practice.

As you'd expect with a group of naturally competitive mechanics, as soon as the rig was installed it immediately became an opportunity for everybody to compete and see who could record the quickest time to complete a wheel change. It wasn't long until even Paul – so calm and tolerant for the most part – grew tired of the noise and had to swing open the office door and bellow, 'Give it a fucking rest'.

Nowadays, when I watch the Formula Two pitstops at the front of the garage, I like to tell myself that I was quicker 'in my day'. Rose-tinted glasses are common when people look back at their careers!

As well as its GP3 entry, in 2011, the following year, Status collaborated with American outfit Level 5 Motorsports to run a Lola LMP2 chassis at Le Mans, the famed twenty-four-hour race that's the crown of the endurance racing calendar. The car would be built and prepped in the Status workshop in Silverstone, with some of the team's US-based personnel coming over to support the build and preparation. Paul told me there was an opportunity for me to be involved in the project if I wished, meaning that I would work on both that and GP3 simultaneously. It was a golden opportunity.

I didn't know the details at the time, but Level 5 Motorsports and its owner, Scott Tucker, were eventually revealed to be facing some serious legal trouble. Many years later, Scott found himself sentenced to a long stretch in a federal prison in the US. There's a 2018 episode of the Netflix series *Dirty Money* about Scott Tucker that I highly recommend if you want to know more about it – one of the cars that we built is actually featured in it. We were aware that there were issues for Tucker back in the US. The mechanics that came over to support the project told us that they would arrive at their workshop and sometimes there would be chains on the doors and legal notices. They said that, each time, Tucker or his lawyers would eventually show up, the doors would be unlocked, and they'd go back to work like nothing had happened. The amount of money spent on the Le Mans project seemed absurd too. The chief mechanic seemed to have an open cheque-book to get any and every tool or piece of equipment we wanted. I guess we now know why.

When I agreed to take on the work, I didn't know much about endurance racing and I'd never worked on anything even similar to an LMP2 car. But I took some advice that Paul had given me only a few months earlier and I agreed to juggle both the European Le Mans Series (ELMS) and GP3 that year. I now always offer the following advice that Paul gave me when I discuss careers with young mechanics: 'If somebody asks you if you can do something, the answer is always yes.' On occasion, this advice might drop you in the deep end but, even so, at least you've given yourself the opportunity to figure it out. With the sport having such a competitive job market, being in the room is almost always a better option than not being there because you hesitated to grab an opportunity.

Juggling both GP3 and LMP2 testing in the build up to the team's Le Mans debut was brutal at times. Often, we'd get back from European races and be straight back into the factory to pack up trucks going to Circuit Paul Ricard in France or Circuito de Jerez in Spain for a shakedown or a test session. Despite the fatigue, it was perfect for a twenty-one-year-old with no girlfriend, dependants or real responsibilities other than the work I was putting into my career. It was a baptism of fire that only further fuelled my love for racing.

As soon as the Lola B11 chassis rolled into the workshop I was straight over to get involved. The large carbon mono-coque was like a shiny spanner to a group of magpies, the whole workshop coming over to get a closer look. These cars were far more complex than the GP3 open-wheeled racers I'd become used to, which were similar to those I'd studied at college. The LMP2 car had a whole host of com-puter trickery with hydraulically powered differentials, traction control and pneumatic jacks built into the chassis. The closed cockpit cars even had air conditioning, a neces-sity to control the temperature as the driver sits next to a whole host of batteries and control units.

Having spent a year learning the ins and outs of the Dallara GP3 chassis, the absolutely awful Renault 2.0-litre turbocharged engine, a basic Hewland sequential gearbox and a hydraulics system, I was ready to get my teeth stuck into something new. I was also excited to learn a new form of racing – the format, the rules and the technical regulations. As an added bonus, to be starting off with the race that's considered the crown of the World Endurance Championship calendar couldn't have been any further into the deep end.

The 24 Hours of Le Mans in 2011 was probably the toughest race I've ever done. By the time you've done the week of testing you're already absolutely shattered. As the team's first ever Le Mans, it was absolute chaos. The workload was immense and we were constantly battling issues that we hadn't predicted. With it being a new team, car and equipment, it was just relentless. Mechanics fatigue wasn't protected against by the curfew periods we enjoy in Formula One today, and any health and safety executive or employee-rights representative would have been appalled by the hours we worked.

As an outfit, we were also largely unpopular in the WEC paddock. I think this was due to the fact that, even though we were a new team, we'd arrived in Le Mans with every piece of equipment you could ask for, a shiny new garage built by Showtrax and a seemingly unlimited budget. This rubbed a few of the less well-funded veteran teams up the wrong way, and I'm sure they took great pleasure in Mr Tucker's fall from grace later on.

By the time the race began on 11 June, I'd already been awake for the best part of thirty hours. I'd been left in charge of dealing with all parts and spares for the car, running the spares truck, taking parts deliveries and keeping a record of everything fitted to the car. While it wasn't initially what I thought would be my dream job, it turned out to be a great way of acquiring some new skills. Firstly, it meant that I got to handle every part of the car, and in turn take the opportunity to learn a bit about each component. It also allowed me plenty of time to take in the atmosphere of my first ever visit to Le Mans. I explored the paddock, met people, and very nearly ran Jackie Stewart over with a golf buggy. I was reversing around the back of a truck and only narrowly avoided him while he was standing there giving an interview. Jackie had survived driving in ninety-nine Grands Prix and was famous for his concerns for driver safety, and I nearly killed him with a golf buggy.

Dealing with the spares was also the first time I'd had to do any administrative work in relation to a race car. Keeping track of parts used in each session and recording mileages were all valuable learning. Now, in my role at Red Bull, I'd estimate that around 50 per cent of my job is administrative work. Even as technicians and mechanics, in modern racing, these skills are now essential if you want to secure a job at the highest level. With the complexity of modern cars and the manufacturing processes required to build them, the job consists of way more than just turning spanners.

Finally, and most importantly to me, the project's chief mechanic, Mark 'Chitty' Chittenden, had asked me if I wanted to be involved in the pit crew. You can probably guess what my answer was. He didn't get to the end of the sentence.

Endurance racing pitstops will always be amazing to me: the sequence of events, the refuelling, the driver swaps . . . so much fun. There was also something special about doing it all throughout the night, under floodlights at 2 a.m. It still feels special now at the night races like Singapore and Las Vegas in the F1 pitlane. I took on the responsibility of doing the driver swap, leaning into the cockpit to help the driver to tighten belts, plug in radios and connect drinks hoses. I was pretty good at it too. At that age, I was still fairly skinny and my long arms were suited to reaching across the cockpit. I imagine my 98-kg self would probably struggle a little bit in that role now.

Level 5 completed 319 laps at that year's Le Mans and finished in tenth overall – a few places ahead of Giancarlo Fisichella's Ferrari – so it was a pretty good result.

My nearly two-year stint at Status was probably the most important part of my career in terms of how quickly I learned so much. I often say now that 'every day is a school day' but it really was the case then, and I was fortunate to be with the team at the perfect time. One of the joys of STEM careers is that because technological progress is constantly being made, there's always more to learn if you want to. It's this period of my life that makes me such an advocate for more apprenticeships in the engineering and motorsport sectors. Being able to earn while learning was crucial to my success. As I'd had to go to college three days a week and then spend the rest of the time trying to get racing, I'd already had to go back to living off my parents and earning cash in any free time that I had. Building-site labouring, fixing people's cars outside their houses on the street and doing pretty much anything for those first nine months or so had taken their toll. I was desperate to get back to earning and having a full-time job, even if just on an apprentice's salary.

My time at Status came to an end when my first Formula One opportunity presented itself rather out of the blue. One day while at work in 2012, my phone rang. It was a number that I didn't recognise. The voice on the other end introduced themselves as Dave O'Neill, team manager at Marussia Formula One team.

Dave explained that he was calling because the team was looking for a factory-based sub-assembly technician and that a friend of his, Simon, who'd been the team manager at Status when I'd first joined the team, had recommended that he call me and ask if I'd like to come and interview for the role. The call was unexpected for sure, but even more so because I hadn't applied for any jobs. I was enjoying my time at Status and I was surprised to hear that it was Simon who'd recommended me as I'd always had the impression that he never particularly liked me. Regardless, I once again took Paul Bellringer's usually sound advice and said 'Absolutely'.

As I'd been taken by surprise by the call, my typically cynical mind's first thought when it ended was that perhaps the whole thing was a practical joke that my colleagues were playing. Perhaps I'd rock up unannounced at the reception of a Formula One team tomorrow for a job that didn't exist. Thinking back on it now, it would have been pretty funny.

Once I'd established that it probably wasn't a practical joke, I then wondered if perhaps a disgruntled Simon had hoped that if I took a job right at the beginning of the season at another team it would disrupt Status and inconvenience Paul by forcing him to find a replacement at short notice. A few months prior, the team had been downsizing and the owners had decided that they didn't need both a team manager and a chief mechanic, and so Paul had taken on both roles, making Simon redundant. It seemed the more likely scenario, rather than just believing that I was actually a decent motorsport mechanic.

As I'd arranged the interview for the following day, during my lunchbreak, I needed to go and tell 'The Angry Pirate' what was going on. I'd be lying if said I wasn't a little nervous walking into the Status GP race office on some idle

Tuesday, just before the start of a season, to tell Paul that I might be jumping ship to another job. But I had to do it. It's not the same as when you work for a big company, where you'd be inclined to keep other opportunities to yourself until you had to hand in your notice. My relationship with Paul had always been a very honest one. I knew that if I was offered the job, I'd have no choice but to take it: I couldn't pass up the opportunity. I also knew that the timing would be an inconvenience. I'm also big on loyalty, sometimes to a fault. I've always felt that if somebody puts faith in you and gives you the opportunity and support to excel, that needs to be something that you value and repay. In a situation like this one, I couldn't help that an opportunity arose when it did, but I could at least be as forthcoming and honest as possible with someone who had helped me to get to this position.

It turned out that I didn't need to be worried walking into that race office at all. In his usual fashion, Paul instantly made me feel at ease about it. He knew what the opportunity meant for me and my career, and if he was even the tiniest bit annoyed, he never showed it. He explained that these opportunities don't come around every day and so, regardless of the circumstances, I had to go for it.

Prior to me going off for my interview the following day, Paul reminded me again of a crucial piece of advice he'd given me: 'Cal, if he asks you if you can do something, what's the answer?'

'Always yes!' I replied.

Needless to say, following this piece of advice, I embellished a little when talking about my skillset during my interview at Marussia. To be perfectly honest, Dave O'Neill could have asked me if I had any experience in orangutan yoga or snake milking, and my answer would have still been, 'Yes, absolutely'.

I remember driving back to the Status workshop after the interview, quietly confident about how it had gone but still quite overwhelmed at how massive and different Formula One teams seemed compared to the small outfits I'd been used to.

When I returned, Paul was eagerly waiting to see how I'd got on. He was listed as my most recent reference on the CV I had provided to Dave O'Neill and I remember him joking that I better be on my best behaviour for the next couple of weeks, just in case someone called him to check if I was even half as good as I'd claimed in my interview.

It wasn't until well after I'd started at Marussia that Dave told me that he had called Paul to learn a little more about me. Dave told me that, in all his time employing motorsport mechanics, he had never received a reference as glowing as the one Paul Bellringer had given me. Apparently, Paul had finished the call by saying, 'Dave, when you and Formula One have broken Calum and he's had enough of it all, can you send him back my way, please? Good mechanics are hard to come by!'

I can't stress enough how grateful I am to Paul for that, or how proud I was that he felt that way about my work. It was high praise indeed and it made me even more determined not to let him down. When I bump into Paul on my travels now, in a pitlane or airport (yes, he is still out there keeping young mechanics on the straight and narrow), I love recounting the laughs and the 'lessons' that sometimes I learned the hard way.

Having been fortunate to have had Paul's great guidance early in my career inspires me to try and have that same impact on the next generation of people who will go on to have incredibly rewarding careers in racing. People who actually give a shit about helping you succeed can be hard to come by sometimes, especially in a workshop of competitive mechanics. Paul is proof that those people do exist and, if you are lucky enough to have them in your life, you must listen to them, learn from their lessons, and understand that the knowledge you can gain from these people cannot be bought or taught in a classroom.

CHAPTER 4

The Big Break

Manor Motorsport was first granted entry into Formula One in 2010. The team had been founded by former single-seater champion John Booth in 1990 and had been successfully competing in Formula Renault and the F3 Euroseries. It boasted being the former home of Lewis Hamilton and Kimi Räikkönen as juniors on their journey to becoming Formula One world champions. The team had secured investment from the likes of Lloyds Banking Group in order to fund its F1 entry and, soon after, Richard Branson confirmed that Virgin had acquired the naming rights so that 'Virgin Racing', rather than 'Manor', would be the newest name on the Formula One grid in 2010.

It was an ambitious project. The VR-01 would be the first modern Formula One car to hit the track having not been tested in a wind tunnel. Technical director Nick Wirth and his team at Wirth Research would aim to design the aerodynamic surfaces of the car using only computational fluid dynamics (CFD) to analyse the aerodynamic design of the car.

The project didn't get off to a great start, when the team discovered early on that the car didn't have a large enough fuel cell to complete a full race distance without there being a long safety car period. The team also suffered from hydraulic problems and a whole host of other issues to be expected from a new team. The team were at a great disadvantage when trying to fix these problems as they had the smallest budget of any outfit on the grid. In 2010, with a budget of only £40 million when the top teams were spending in excess of £200 million, Richard Branson was quoted as saying, 'Money's not everything'. He was wrong. This is Formula One, and even in today's 'cost-capped' era, money is still everything!

After two unsuccessful seasons, Wirth and Branson cut their losses and the team was fully rebranded as Marussia F1 team in 2012, competing under a Russian licence and receiving funding as a subsidiary of the now defunct Moscow-based Marussia supercar manufacturer.

For the 2013 season, the team fielded cars to be driven by Max Chilton and Jules Bianchi, both of whom had joined after working their way up through the ranks of the junior formulas. Max had been involved with Marussia-backed

Carlin Motorsport throughout his time in GP2, and Jules was a Ferrari junior and a star on the rise.

Despite the team becoming the first Russian-licensed manufacturer to score points in Formula One, thanks to Jules Bianchi's incredible late dive down the inside at Rascasse at the 2014 Monaco GP, it was a team that seemed destined to forever be a 'backmarker'. We all knew that we'd be seeing plenty of blue flags before the chequered one each week. The project never seemed likely to survive in the long run without finding a way to bring in more investment. Unfortunately, despite the best efforts of John Booth and CEO Graeme Lowdon, the team succumbed to administration just prior to the 2014 US GP, along with back-of-the-field rival, Caterham.

Based in a comparatively modest factory in Banbury, Oxfordshire, the same one now occupied by the Haas F1 team, things weren't often easy at Marussia but, in hindsight, I'm glad that they weren't. It was an excellent environment for me to learn the sport. With little expectation in terms of results and, with that, no real pressure on me, it was the perfect place for me to grow in confidence and push myself. That's not to suggest for a second that the effort put in by those in the garage was any less than our distant rivals. We took great pride in being the most reliable car on the grid throughout the 2013 season, although we did use to joke that it was simply because we weren't going fast enough for anything to break.

One thing that I try to impress on mechanics, after asking them about their career aspirations, is that no opportunity in a Formula One team is too small or insignificant. So many of the aspiring technicians I talk to seem to have a definitive picture of where they want to end up, but very little idea of the importance of the journey they need to make to get there.

My time at Marussia Formula One Team, while not littered with on-track success, was a key part of my journey to achieving all of the goals I'd set out for myself back in 2009. It is where I learned a multitude of technical skills related to running a Formula One car as well as a foundational understanding of the politics of the sport and the inner workings of the paddock. It was a time similar to my spell at Ridge Garage, where I took on so much knowledge, so quickly, that I consider it as one of the pivotal periods in my career.

It's a lesson that any opportunity is only worth what you choose to get out of it, and if you find yourself in the position of being offered a role in a smaller or 'backmarker' team, take it. Starting from the bottom in any discipline is rarely a bad thing. All of the best mechanics and technicians I've worked with over the years cut their teeth at small, low-budget teams in feeder series.

When people tell me that their aim is to work for a particular team, I tell them that while that is a perfectly good long-term goal, in the shorter term, being more open-minded about the roles that they might be interested in is an approach that is far more likely to lead to success. Getting a foot into the F1 paddock, regardless of which team it is with, is a far more sensible strategy than focusing all your efforts on one particular role that likely has thousands of applicants.

My own career is a pretty good example of this. As a general rule, I took any and every opportunity to go racing that came my way. If I could physically achieve it without having to master time travel or teleportation, I would do it. I travelled long distances, slept in my car and did whatever it took to be racing and networking. My experience is that if you do this, those opportunities will keep coming, I don't think I ever turned down an offer to take on something new until I was well into my time at Red Bull.

I arrived at Marussia in 2012, a young No. 2 mechanic with a general understanding of race cars and how they worked, but little specialist knowledge. The LMP2 car was the only vehicle I had ever worked on that was anything close to the more refined engineering of Formula One. Taking on a factory-based sub-assembly role, I soon started to pick up more specific and detailed knowledge about gearboxes, suspension assemblies, wheel guns, fuel systems and all manner of other things.

As sub-assembly was just a three-man department, it was a great way to see and learn about almost every assembly on the car. We didn't have the resources that I'm accustomed to now, where car assembly is split into multiple departments with not only many technicians, but a plethora of people dealing with all the administrative work. I often impress on the apprentices we have at Red Bull just how spoiled we are now and try to pass on the skills that are often forgotten as a result of the privilege of modern workshops and processes.

It was busy, and the team was just me, a lead technician and an apprentice. During the weeks that the race team were back from a Grand Prix and we were turning the cars around, I'd often expect to work well over my contracted hours every day, trying to get all of the jobs done. Often, for those four or five days, I'd drive back home down the M40 at midnight, only to be leaving home at six-thirty the following morning. During the weeks that the team were away and the workload dipped, I'd recoup those hours by clocking off in the early afternoon most days. It was a pretty good deal. That kind of flexibility is something usually you only see in small businesses. It's certainly not like that now. Hours worked are rigorously logged and production departments manage how the workload is allocated among the technicians.

While my goal was still to get to the racetrack, I loved the work in sub-assembly. I liked the organisation of it all. I liked understanding the assemblies and learning the techniques required to service them, and I liked feeding back to the design office about how we could improve them. There's something very satisfying about sub-assembly work: starting the day with trays full of parts and finishing with a desk that's got a load of complete assemblies lined up across it, all of them new and built identically. While now I dread the perceived banality of factory life, I enjoyed the work back then. A few months into the job, when I was asked if I'd like to fill the rear-end No. 2 mechanic role on the race team, that learning curve began all over again.

I've always tried to be malleable and willing to adapt as necessary to any new opportunity to progress, rather than waiting for a role that I thought would be 'perfect' for me. As an example, before the opportunity arose to join the race team at Red Bull as an engine assembly technician, I'd barely done any engine assembly work at all. Always consider how what you can learn from an opportunity that is available to you right now, despite being imperfect, can benefit you in reaching your long-term goals.

Inside the small Banbury workshop, Dave O'Neill had assembled a pretty good crew of mechanics and technicians, some of whom I went on to work alongside at Red Bull, while others ended up in senior roles at the other big teams in the paddock. I guess, much like for drivers, the small teams like Marussia and backmarker rival Caterham almost acted as an unofficial academy for the larger, well-funded outfits. It was the perfect place for young mechanics to learn the sport and build themselves a reputation, putting themselves in a great position to advance their careers. The smaller teams provided a great stepping stone into a sector that was otherwise hard to break into.

At the time, having F1 experience on your CV seemed to be the only way to have a chance of securing an F1 job. The apprenticeships and student programmes that most teams offer today didn't exist back then. Pathways into the sport were few and far between, and nepotism was rife. The few Formula One jobs that were on offer were advertised in *Autosport* with an often vague description, but almost always with the caveat 'previous F1 or equivalent experience required'. This, of course, led to the age-old issue of how to gain experience without being eligible to gain experience. This conundrum is one that students face every day as they transition from education to employment – it happens in almost every industry. For me, Marussia, a relatively small and largely unknown team, solved this problem.

Marussia certainly operated like a small team in comparison to what I later experienced and I was reminded of this in 2024 when a discussion about the gap between teams' resources under the sport's new financial regulations came to the fore. In an interview, James Vowles, team principal at Williams, revealed that when he took on the role, the team were still using endless pages of Microsoft Excel spreadsheets to account for their stock of parts. The story put into perspective the gap between teams at either end of the grid in terms of operational resources even in today's cost-capped Formula One. Nearly a decade after I'd had to use a similar never-ending series of spreadsheets to keep tabs on the service schedules of wheel guns and bearing assemblies back in the three-person sub-assembly department at Marussia, the idea that Williams was still building a race car that way was absurd. By comparison, the sport's top teams have myriad intricate business systems and clever software to manage the hundreds of thousands of parts, as well as an army of production, logistics and parts-management personnel to oversee the task.

This was exactly the kind of disparity that we were up against at Marussia. You felt like you couldn't win. Comparing the resources and investment between ourselves and Red Bull or Ferrari, for example, it was a struggle to believe that we were even competing in the same sport as those challenging for wins every week. For us, eighteenth place, or anywhere in front of the Caterham cars, was about the best result we could expect. Jules Bianchi's ninth-place finish at the 2014 Monaco Grand Prix felt like a win for us. It was one of those cathartic moments where you feel like all the work is worth it.

By the time I started at Red Bull Racing, I understood all too well that the gap between the teams at the two opposite ends of the paddock wasn't really a 'gap' at all, it was a chasm. I used to joke that the reason Marussia couldn't win was that everyone else was cheating somehow and we weren't. In reality, there was just no way to improve beyond your competitors without all of the tools they had at their disposal, and as this was prior to the cost cap, the big teams could always spend more than we could.

The disadvantages we faced weren't just related to the design and build of the car either. We also didn't have the number of people required to operate in the same way as the big teams. At Marussia, there were only a couple of hundred staff. When I joined Red Bull in 2015, the number was around seven or eight hundred. Today, with all of its different entities, the Red Bull technology campus alone hosts around 1,500 people. It is a huge business.

Nowadays, at Red Bull Racing, most race-team personnel are given days in lieu throughout the weeks that they're home between races. The mechanics and technicians only go into the factory for one day between events, often just for pitstop practice. In all honesty, we'd like it to be none at all. Most of the front-running teams are blessed with factory departments dedicated to re-prepping the cars prior to the next event. At Marussia, we were lucky if we even managed to get one or two days off before repacking the air freight or the trucks and flying to the next event. It was brutal. With much shorter curfew periods than we have now, unfavourable flights to reduce costs and no prospect of winning, the disparity between the top and bottom of the paddock felt, sort of, unfair.

It didn't really matter, though. I still loved it. I was twenty-three and earning £45,000 a year plus expenses while flying around the world building race cars and partying. What was not to love?

The reason why I always encourage people to get involved in motorsports as early as possible isn't because you can't achieve your goals as you get older. I say it because if you decide that a travelling role is the goal, starting before you have a long list of responsibilities makes it so much easier. What I learned very quickly at Marussia was that Formula One, as opposed to GP3, ELMS and all of the other racing I'd done so far, was going to be all-consuming. When I was at Status, and even for the time I was factory-based before joining the race team at Marussia, I had a pretty normal life outside of the working hours one might expect at any job. As much as it pains me to use the old cliché 'It's not a job, it's a lifestyle', I really do struggle to find a better way to describe what it's like as a travelling mechanic in F1. Starting before you've really shaped the rest of your life makes it far simpler to build your life around it. Had it not been for the job, I wouldn't have met my amazing partner, Phoebe, though, and had our daughter, Isabella. So, while now at the ripe old age of thirty-five the long calendar is a rather great burden on the life I've built, at twenty-three, the nomadic lifestyle was perfect.

I suppose, like most unexpectedly great things, Marussia couldn't last for ever. While we'd all become used to the inconveniences of working in a team with financial struggles, by the time the 2014 season began, it felt like from one week to the next there was some new threat to the survival of the team. The collapse of the business had felt imminent for some time. It had probably begun even before I'd started. In my very first week in sub-assembly there had been a shortage of brake cleaner. I was told that stores had run out and, due to debts owed, the team had struggled to find a supplier willing to take on any more liability. These incidents came in waves over the next year or so. I imagined to myself that every few months an unmarked duffle bag of Russian cash would arrive, and that's what would tide us over for a little while.

The severity of the situation became apparent when we landed in Belgium that year and received an email from human resources telling us that the team wasn't going to be able to pay our wages on time that month. It wasn't lost on us that the email had been sent (seemingly deliberately) a few minutes after our flight had departed the UK. With us now already in Belgium, I suppose the logic was that we'd work on regardless as the team being unable to compete would have only worsened the crisis. A few prominent voices in the garage made it clear that unless they were paid, however, they would down tools. When that Friday arrived, mysteriously, we were all paid. The rumour among the mechanics was that Max Chilton's dad had paid our wages that month, but I've never asked Max to confirm if that was true. This incident was probably the first that made me think that Marussia weren't going to survive as a Formula One team beyond the season.

My time at Marussia, while being so important to the progress of my career, is unfortunately also a painful reminder of one of my worst days in racing. Jules Bianchi's crash in our car at the Japanese Grand Prix, on the afternoon of Sunday 5 October 2014, changed for ever my appreciation for the importance of everything we do in regard to safety at a racetrack.

The 2014 Japanese Grand Prix was a disaster from the outset. The rain caused by an inbound typhoon had begun before the cars had even left the garages to head to the grid. As we were on the grid, the rain got even worse and, as we waited for a delayed start to the race, it should have been apparent that there was little to no chance of conditions improving enough for the race to be run without incident. As the race began behind the safety car and all twenty-two cars tiptoed their way around the circuit, it became immediately clear that the circuit was not suitable to race on, with huge patches of standing water and multiple cars spinning off behind the safety car. Sebastian Vettel told his team on the radio that he was aquaplaning at 180 km/h and all of the drivers were complaining that visibility was very poor. After two laps behind the safety car, the red flags came out and the race was halted.

That should have been the end of the 2014 Japanese Grand Prix. But as the rain began to ease, the decision was taken to go again. While the rainfall slowed and then worsened intermittently throughout the next thirty or so laps, the visibility for anyone following a car closely was awful due to all the spray from the standing water being kicked up. The rain began to increase again around lap 40 and the sky got incredibly dark. Driver complaints about conditions were seemingly being ignored, and many of us in the garage were in disbelief that the race hadn't been red flagged. Then, on lap 43, Adrian Sutil lost control of his Sauber on the outside of turn 7 and hurtled towards the barriers, bringing out the yellow flags in that sector.

Looking up at the menacingly dark sky from the pitlane, the rain seemed to have worsened and the patches of standing water through the usually fast corners of sector 1 were now a river, visibly flowing down the tarmac. In an effort to remove the stricken Sauber car from the barriers, a recovery vehicle, in the form of a tractor, had been driven into the gravel trap in the yellow-flag sector to lift and remove the damaged car.

One lap later, although he'd reduced his speed as required by the yellow-flag rules at the time, Jules Bianchi hit a patch of standing water, aquaplaned and careered off the track on the exit of turn 7, hitting the recovery vehicle at high speed. The data showed that Jules had put more than 60 bar of pressure through the brake pedal in an effort to prevent the impact. Unfortunately, from the moment he hit the standing water, he was a passenger.

I was not in any way prepared, at the age of twenty-four, to have been responsible for building a car that somebody later died in. Regardless of the cause of the crash not being a mechanical fault, the guilt of having been one of the mechanics responsible for that car broke me for a little while.

When we visit Japan now, even ten years later, whenever it rains I can't help but vividly recall the events of that day.

Subsequently, as much as I love Japan, it can be a tough week for me. As a race mechanic, whenever your car is involved in a crash on track, your usual first reaction tends to be disappointment or anger. Both of these emotions, while understandable, are actually a luxury. They are a result of our familiarity with the overall safety of a modern Formula One car. We're all so used to seeing drivers walk away unscathed from incredibly big impacts that perhaps we forget in those moments what it took to get us to this level of safety.

Since Jules's crash in Japan, which ultimately cut short his life, we've seen safety standards in the sport improve in almost every area. Many of these improvements are a direct result of learning from that crash in Japan, 2014. The most obvious of those changes was the introduction of the 'halo', the frame around the top of the cockpit designed to protect the driver's head. The head injuries that cost Jules his life, while far from guaranteed, could potentially have been lessened if the cars back then provided the same protection that they do now.

Among many fans of the sport and commentators alike, the introduction of the halo was initially an unpopular addition to the cars. People largely felt that the halo wasn't particularly pleasing from an aesthetic point of view and, while those voices weren't necessarily wrong, it seems absurd now to think that head protection for the drivers of open-cockpit race cars could have been overlooked for so long. Even when we look at some of the on-track incidents in the last few years, so many of them could have ended differently had the halo not been a safety feature of car design since 2018. Zhou Guanyu's long drag across the tarmac and through the gravel, upside down, on his way to the barriers outside of turn 1 at Silverstone, at the start of the 2022 British GP, is just one example of the halo's effectiveness. Another example is the now infamous images of Max Verstappen and Lewis Hamilton's collision in Monza in 2021. Both of these crashes, along with many others that we've seen since the introduction of the halo, could have had far grimmer outcomes had the sport not learned from Jules's crash.

As well as car design, the sport has also changed its operational practices with safety in mind. The introduction of the virtual safety car (VSC) now allows race control to neutralise a race with minimal negative impact, allowing stricken vehicles to be recovered more safely. As well as this, new rules pertaining to the use of recovery vehicles were introduced. Along with Pierre Gasly, I was also horrified to see a recovery vehicle on the circuit without warning during the 2022 Japanese Grand Prix. Seeing the footage during that red-flag period triggered all those memories of 2014 for me. Now, drivers are always given prior warning from race control on the radio whenever there's a recovery vehicle on the track.

There also seems to be a far more cautious approach taken when severe weather impacts visibility, another factor in Jules's crash. I know that it frustrates fans that race control rarely allows racing to continue beyond a mild amount of rainfall now, but you need to understand that it's really not worth it. There's nothing courageous about putting yourself or others in a potentially life-threatening situation.

Safety in motor racing, much like performance development, is an ever-evolving philosophy. Unfortunately, as with so many that have lost their lives racing, the sport's safety measures at the time just weren't evolved enough to save Jules's life. He was a great guy, always smiling, humble and appreciative of all he had in life. When Jules used to walk around the Marussia garage and ask people how they were, you got the impression that he actually cared. It wasn't just something that his manager had told him to do, like a chore. Jules wanted to be a part of the crew, he wanted to know about your life, and he appreciated the work we were doing for him. The last photograph of Jules and me that was posted to his Instagram captured a memory that I hold very dearly. A conversation about a friend that turned into a challenge to see how many Ty-Raps I could store in my hair, and the laughs that came with it . . . it's a fitting way for me to remember Jules and the smile he wore so frequently.

As I said, as a race mechanic, frustration is usually the emotion that sums up your weekend if your car was involved in a shunt. However, when you know that your car has been involved in a serious incident, due to a previously unseen danger, the emotion that takes over is always horror, sheer horror. You get that stomach-sinking feeling, like the earth is about to swallow you whole and, despite every muscle in your body twitching simultaneously, you can't move. When it happens, you find yourself desperately waiting for relief, as though you're being suffocated. That first glimpse of relief, that hope, usually comes in the form of a radio message. A reply to the most important question an engineer will ever ask a driver. In 2014, that question came from the voice of race engineer Dave Greenwood. 'Are you OK?' It's the only thing that matters in that moment, the only thing that can give you relief from that sinking feeling. You wait, and wait. But each time you hear 'Are you OK?' and it's met with a deafening silence, you sink further.

I had already experienced one of those tense, worried moments prior to my time at Marussia. Back when I was doing ELMS, I'd been a mechanic on Alexander Sims's Lola B11 when he had an almighty shunt in qualifying at Spa, at the top of Eau Rouge. Due to the layout of Spa, when Alex hadn't responded to his 'Are you OK?' message, we were able to run out of the back of the garage and, to our relief, see him moving and getting out of the destroyed chassis. The radio wiring had been damaged in the crash, leaving Alex unable to respond.

When Jules didn't respond in Japan, I had a little moment of denial where I remembered that other crash and I told myself the same had probably just happened. But that denial didn't last long and the realisation that the accident was severe hit the garage like nothing I've experienced since.

I had to go, with my car crew, to recover Jules's chassis from the FIA garage that evening, and the image will be ingrained in my mind for ever. I'd never seen anything like it. From the moment we uncovered the chassis, we knew that nobody could have survived an impact that violent. The 'survival cell', the carbon fibre monocoque chassis that has the primary purpose of protecting the driver in an impact, didn't even look as though it was a big enough space for an adult human to fit into any more. My heart broke. I somehow managed to make it outside the back of the FIA garage before completely breaking down. I sat there for the entire time that the rest of the paddock was packing up, and just cried.

The weeks that followed were a complete blur. The following morning, after Japan, we flew directly to Sochi for the inaugural Russian GP. This was another one of the toughest weeks of my life. Physically and emotionally drained, I just wanted to go home and curl up on the sofa. I didn't want to be anywhere near a racetrack. I didn't even want to think about racing, let alone unpack the air freight and build a race car. Furthermore, I was about to learn a harsh reality about the ruthless relationship between the business and the sport, under Formula One's previous management.

When we arrived at the track in Russia, we'd already been told by the team's management that we had no plans to run Jules's car that week. We planned to build the car, using the spare chassis, and leave it in the garage for the weekend as a tribute to Jules. It was the right decision. Neither I nor anyone else on the crew was in the right frame of mind to be able to do our jobs competently. In any other line of work, there's no doubt that we would have been signed off on compassionate leave. We were told that our reserve driver, Alexander Rossi, was also not particularly keen to drive that week, understandably. What I wasn't expecting was that choosing not to run the car that week, given the circumstances, would be an issue for anyone. However, it was apparently a problem for the sport's management under Bernie Ecclestone.

During that Wednesday leading up to the Russian GP, through the usual grapevine of gossip that trickles through any team, we were told that we may have to run the car after all. I'd been building rear-ends in the garage and throughout the day there had been various senior figures from Formula One Management, including Bernie himself, coming in and out to speak to team owner John Booth and other senior management figures. While this didn't seem unusual in itself under the circumstances, as the day went on, it became apparent that some of these conversations were less than friendly. It didn't appear like a situation where people were popping in to give their condolences for the tragedy that had occurred just three days' prior.

It wasn't until later on that day that I was told that the reason we may have to run the car was because, apparently, the sport's management had told John Booth that if we didn't run the car, the team could be fined. Someone that was privy to the conversation quoted Bernie as saying,

'People have paid to see twenty-two cars.' At first, I didn't really believe it. It's tough to think that somebody might be so callous, so uncaring, so completely focused on the impact something might have on their profits, and have so little regard for those personally affected by a tragedy. Now, more worldly-wise and appreciative of how often business and sport collide in this manner, it doesn't surprise me at all that somebody could be so completely devoid of empathy that they might make such a threat.

With that said, Marussia were never fined for us not running the car that week. My guess is that even though social media wasn't as powerful a tool back then, the potential for bad press coverage if we had been fined was just too great of a risk. I suppose the other option is that Bernie ultimately had the self-awareness to realise he shouldn't risk being seen as a prick, but I doubt it to be honest.

Jules's crash is one of the very few things about my time in the sport that I genuinely struggle to speak about. I hate when people ask me about it. The truth is, there are still things about that day that I'm unhappy with, one of those being that I feel nobody was ever truly held to account for some of the decisions made that day. In my view, the decision to continue that race in spite of the conditions was reckless and it cost a man his life. I'm angry that Jules had to be driven to hospital, rather than airlifted, as the conditions were so bad that the helicopter couldn't fly. Any doctor will tell you the importance of time when getting a casualty to hospital with severe head injuries. Jules was let down. I believe that on that day in 2014, a conscious decision was made to place entertainment over safety.

So, while I'll always be glad to see how Jules's legacy will forever play a huge role in keeping drivers safe today, that day at Suzuka will forever be my worst memory of the sport that I love.

No. 1 mechanic Kieron Marchant called me nine months later, in July 2015, to tell me that Jules had died from the injuries he'd sustained. Jules was never going to recover, so at least this was some form of closure – to be able to think that our friend's ordeal was over, and that he was finally at peace.

Japan seemed to hang over the team for the rest of its existence. It changed the atmosphere in the garage completely. Understandably, we were no longer the same group of enthusiastic and driven mechanics; our friend was in a serious and critical condition, a lot of us could now see that the team was collapsing financially, and some had just completely lost the love for racing. In October 2014, when we were all finally called up to the design office in the Banbury factory one day and told that the company was being placed into administration, in some ways I felt a sense of relief.

Once it became apparent that Marussia was facing imminent collapse, the thought that my Formula One dream might come screeching to an abrupt halt was obviously worrying. I would now find myself in a scramble to find another Formula One job among the hundreds of mechanics and technicians doing the same, many of whom were vastly more experienced than I was and had a much better network within the paddock.

I considered at the time how happy I had been at Status, and whether I should just call up Paul Bellringer and ask him if there was any space for me to go back there, but that would have put a huge dent in my pride. Having made plenty of contacts throughout my time at Status, I also looked at what other opportunities I might find outside of the Formula One paddock. I'd loved my time with the LMP2 car and knew I had the contacts to pursue a path there, but it wasn't my dream. The thought of giving up on something after only two years, after working so hard to get the opportunity in the first place, weighed heavily on my mind.

I also didn't have the time to hang around not earning money. By this point, I'd moved out of my mum's house and into my own flat. I had bills to pay and no income. I needed to get back to work immediately, but I was mentally exhausted and still very emotional about Jules's crash in Suzuka.

It felt entirely unfair that, through no fault of my own, I was again being made redundant by a business I'd given everything to help succeed. This redundancy, however, did feel less personal than the one I'd suffered at Ridge Garage. I think this was because Marussia was a much larger business and because it was happening to everyone, not just me. It was easier to take in that sense, but on the other hand the stakes felt so much higher this time. The problem was that being a backmarker team, I didn't feel as though I'd had any opportunity to really establish myself in the paddock or create any sort of reputation. I also hadn't been in the paddock for long enough to have built any sort of network I could use to find other opportunities.

So I went back to basics. I sent emails and letters, constantly, to every single team in the Formula One paddock. I included a CV, updated with my limited F1 experience and a cover note outlining my willingness to take on any junior role that teams might have available. I then started to call in favours from anyone I knew who had contacts inside Formula One teams. I spent the next couple of months doing this while taking on any contractor work that I came across. In his typically helpful fashion, Paul threw me a bone anywhere he could, doing what's known as 'weekend warrior' work whenever he was short of someone at a race weekend (and to be fair, even when he didn't really need me). It's another addition to the long list of things for which I'll be forever grateful to Paul.

My letters and emails eventually started to get through to teams, and it looked like my persistence might just pay off. Initially, many teams had responded to most of my emails in the usual fashion, explaining that they'd keep my CV on file for the future, but at the current time they didn't have anything suitable available. In some cases, teams just didn't respond at all. It was a terrible time of year to be looking for a Formula One job really, mid-season when most of a team's resources and focus would have been on the current championship.

The first piece of positive news came from Ferrari. This was a good lesson in the importance of networking in motorsport. When I had contacted Ferrari in Maranello, I'd thought it unlikely that I'd get a response. In my head, it seemed unlikely that anyone would consider the hassle of employing someone who didn't currently live in Italy over the thousands of applicants on their doorstep.

What I hadn't counted on was the influence of having worked alongside Ferrari technicians during my time at Marussia. With Marussia having utilised the Italian manufacturer's engine and gearbox for the 2014 season, I'd worked closely with the Ferrari technicians that were embedded within the team, and we had got on well. We'd bonded the way that people who speak different languages often do: they taught me all the 'bad' words in Italian and I shared some of my favourite English expressions. This meant that when someone at Maranello read my correspondence, they had an immediate reference point. They would have gone and spoken to some of the technicians that knew me, and I can only imagine that the feedback was good because it was the first breakthrough that I made in my job hunt.

It happens all the time: a chief mechanic or department manager will read a CV and recognise a workplace because they know someone else that worked there, so they'll go and ask them. Making friends works! Equally, not making enemies is also important. I remember one day in the workshop in Marussia when Dave O'Neill came down to the race bays to ask me if I knew someone who had been contracted by Status while I was there. I did, and the guy was a nightmare. I was just working out the most professional way to deliver this verdict to Dave, without just saying, 'This guy is a complete prick,' when, thankfully, one of the No. 1 mechanics eloquently piped up and said, 'I know him, and if you hire him, I'm quitting.' Needless to say, Dave moved on to the next candidate.

Ferrari, without making any promises, offered to fly me out to Italy for an interview with then chief mechanic, Diego Ioverno. I didn't know Diego personally, so I did what any sensible person would do in this situation: I spoke to some of the Ferrari technicians about my upcoming interview and asked what Diego was like. They imparted to me the importance of passion within the team, explaining that they liked people who wanted to be part of Ferrari's legacy and prestige, and that they were very much like a family in comparison to the rest of the paddock.

I started to think that job opportunities in motorsport were like buses in that you'd wait and wait for one and then three would come along all at once. By the time the day came for me to fly into Bologna, I'd also had a response from Torro Rosso, who'd agreed to interview me over Skype, and then, finally, I'd received a response from Red Bull Racing.

Both had explained that while they didn't currently have any opportunities available, they'd like to build a relationship with me with the future in mind. In the case of Red Bull Racing, they thought that there might be a factory-based position opening up in the new year. First, I had to prepare for Ferrari.

Sitting in the office of Diego Ioverno, among the huge, red, monumental buildings of the Ferrari factory in Maranello, I couldn't help but feel a little nervous. It was one of those times where I felt truly out of my depth, an imposter in a world I didn't belong in. Thankfully, Diego's natural charm was able to put me slightly more at ease once we began talking, and seeing some of the Ferrari technicians that I already knew as I walked through the vast complex helped a little too. It was an amazing experience and there's little doubt that I would have been very happy had I ended up working for Ferrari.

Ultimately, though, both Diego and I knew that I wasn't at a point in my life where I wanted to move to Italy. I was willing, for sure. I was willing to do anything to stay in the sport, but it wasn't ideal for me, and Diego and I had an honest discussion about this. As a result of getting to know one another a little, he said, when I informed him that I was also interviewing for Toro Rosso and Red Bull, that he'd be willing to offer any reference or help that he could in this regard.

Seeing Diego go on to excel in his role as sporting director for the team wasn't surprising to me at all. Even in that brief meeting with him ten years ago, it was instantly apparent that he has exactly the kind of personality that makes a great leader. Now, we always have a kind word for one another passing in the paddock, and Diego is another person on my list of those that I'm truly thankful to have encountered on my journey.

Returning to the UK after my Ferrari interview, I felt inspired. The mental fatigue brought on by the events at Marussia had started to fade and I'd turned a corner in my belief that I would find a role to keep me in this sport that I'd fallen in love with. This newfound exuberance was timed perfectly with my interview at Red Bull Racing, where I was due to sit down with the head of car build, Dave Boys.

Having already worked inside a Formula One facility and interviewed at Ferrari, you'd think that I'd have been well prepared for what to expect, but I really wasn't. I'd left home with plenty of time as I hadn't been able to sleep the night before. Even filling out the last bits of paper-work prior to leaving home for the interview, my hands had been shaking. I now know that the level my nerves reached was pretty ridiculous and that, provided I had carried on with my steadfast, persistent approach, there is little doubt that I would have ended up on a similar path regardless. It just didn't feel that way at the time. I just had this feeling in my gut that this was my last chance, that it was going to be this interview that paved my route to long-term success in racing, or it would be back to the building site.

CHAPTER 5

Red Bull Racing –
The Long Return to Glory

Driving into the Red Bull technology campus in Milton Keynes for the first time, knowing that this was the home of the team that, from 2010 to 2013, had won four consecutive constructors' and drivers' championships in incredible style after being dismissed by some as a 'fizzy-drinks manufacturer', was quite a daunting experience.

Once I'd arrived and checked in at reception for my interview, I was then told that joining Dave Boys and me in the interview would be the support team manager, Tony Burrows, as well as race team chief mechanic, Phil Turner. This was unexpected, to say the least. Having successfully managed to calm myself and mentally prepare for a routine one-to-one job interview, I was now preparing for what would feel like a trial with three of the most influential figures at the team.

Usually in situations like that I would tell myself that the worst that could happen was them saying 'No', at which point I'd be no worse off than before, but I felt as though that wasn't really the case here. I knew that if I bombed this interview, I'd now have three influential figures in the sport who'd be unlikely to hire me in the future, and if any other potential employer in the paddock were to ask them about me, their opinions would hold significant weight.

I don't remember much about what was said during that first interview. I think we spoke broadly about my experience and talked about the people I'd worked with so far, and then Tony asked me the age-old question of why I wanted to work for Red Bull. The only pertinent thing that I do distinctly remember was a question that Dave Boys asked me towards the end of the interview. It's one that people will be familiar with and almost seems clichéd today. He asked me what I wanted from the job and what I'd like to be able to say about it in five years' time.

My response was very clear and honest. I told Dave that I really didn't care about my job title or salary, beyond the need to pay my bills and live comfortably. I explained that I hoped that, in five years' time, I would have fulfilled my major goal, which was to be considered an asset to any team that I worked for, to be known as the guy you could rely on to get the job done under any circumstances and by any means necessary. I didn't actually know a great deal about the team's ethos when I gave that answer. I simply knew that Red Bull were considered to be the 'fun' team to work for.

Looking back, I don't think I could have given a more perfect answer to that question. Valuing people as their greatest assets is, for me, one of the things that sets Red Bull Racing apart from the rest of the Formula One paddock. I can only imagine that the answer I gave to Dave's question proved to be pivotal to his decision about who to recruit for the car build mechanic role.

Sometime during December 2014, I was preparing to go on a family holiday to the Caribbean, trying to escape the dreaded English winter. It was kindly financed by my mum as at this point I was flat broke. I'd not long returned from Abu Dhabi, helping Status as a contractor during the GP3 young driver test that followed the final Formula One race of the season. While sitting on the sofa at home in my flat, the phone rang. Like a lot of people, I'm suspicious of calls from numbers that I don't recognise; sometimes I don't even answer the phone. In this case, it was a good job I did, as the voice at the other end went on to explain that Red Bull Racing would like to offer me the role of car build mechanic, and asked me when I might be able to start. My initial answer was 'Tomorrow', completely forgetting that I was due to go on holiday the following week. Thankfully the team had a January start date in mind, and I would officially join Red Bull Racing on 5 January 2015.

After hanging up the phone I sat in complete silence, alone in the lounge, for at least ten minutes before calling my mother and my partner, Phoebe, to deliver the good news. In truth, it didn't really start to sink in until I received my contract and new-starter paperwork to fill in just prior to Christmas. Needless to say, receiving the news when I did made it one of my best Christmases ever and a blowout holiday at the end of a very difficult year.

When I arrived at the Red Bull campus on 5 January, excited about what this next chapter in Formula One would hold for me, I said to myself in the car, '*This* is how you get your fucking championship'. It was one of those very specific memories in my life that feels like a defining moment. A moment of reflection where I reminded myself that I'd achieved each of the short-term targets that I'd set myself to get to this point, and that now I needed to refocus and go for that ultimate goal of winning a World Constructors' Championship.

Something that I'd realised during my time at Marussia, which perhaps I'd never considered before, was that throughout the history of the sport, tens of thousands of great mechanics had passed their entire careers without having had the opportunity to win a constructors' championship. Being in the right place at the right time was just as important as being good at the work if winning a championship was the goal. I couldn't get caught up in my head thinking about anything other than the here and now, so I decided to continue setting myself achievable short-term targets.

The race team had a very clear structure and pathway set out for mechanics wanting to work trackside. From where I would start, as a factory-based car build No. 2 mechanic, I needed to get a role on the support team, attending demonstration events with the historic cars and doing nightshifts during pre-season testing. From there, I could put myself in a position to be considered for a race-team role when one became available.

I'd already spent plenty of time trackside, and with the experience of Marussia (the good and the bad) under my belt, I felt like a seasoned F1 mechanic. The role I'd now taken on was essentially a junior one but it was what I needed to do to stay in the sport and get back to the track. I told myself that I could achieve these steps inside three years. It wasn't ideal, but it was realistic. There were other good mechanics ahead of me in this process and the environment was too new for me to be able to assume I'd make it happen any quicker.

By chance, just seven days after I'd started in car build, some shuffling of personnel gave me the opportunity to move over to the support team. Then, midway through 2015, I covered for Daniel Ricciardo's rear-end mechanic for two races, Monaco and Canada, while he was on paternity leave. I made sure that I got the most out of the trackside opportunity, getting the job done with the intention that the rest of the garage would hardly notice the change in personnel. Keeping my head down isn't something I'm particularly well-known for now, but back then it was imperative. With these few chances to shine, I'd put myself in a position to be the natural choice for a permanent race-team role when one became available during the 2016 season.

At the end of 2015, the 'engine kitter' – the person responsible for fitting pipework and exhausts to engines at the circuit – left and I was encouraged to apply for the role by then support-team chief mechanic Joe Robinson. At this point in my career, I'd effectively never assembled a Formula One engine at all. I'd never had to, apart from fitting the odd water or oil pipe when installing an engine into a chassis. In GP3, the engines used to arrive from the manufacturer, in a box, already assembled. At Marussia, Cosworth had taken care of the V8 for the most part and then the Ferrari technicians had dealt with the customer V6 hybrid power unit in the 2014 season, so I'd really never paid that much attention to engines. I'd been too busy trying to learn my own bits of the car.

With that said, I quickly discovered that rear-end mechanics at Red Bull Racing had it easy compared to what was required at Marussia. At Red Bull, the rear-end mechanics pretty much only have to take care of the outboard suspension and brake installations. At Marussia, as well as all of the assemblies outside of the gearbox casing, the rear-end mechanic would also be responsible for all of the inboard suspension and dampers, something that at Red Bull Racing is taken care of by the hydraulics and gearbox technicians.

I was confident enough to take the job on. I often say to people, 'It's all just nuts and bolts,' and it really is. If you know how to read and follow a technical drawing, and you have the tools, it doesn't really matter what it is you're building. Those old Royal Navy adverts on the TV that said something along the lines of 'if you can repair this skateboard, then you can repair this F-35 Lightning' weren't as farfetched as they may have seemed. I like to think that anyone can learn to do the job. Assembling any part of a race car with the technical information and parts required is often far easier than diagnosing and repairing the average road car. A good race car is designed to be worked on and repaired quickly. So I wasn't at all concerned about understanding how to do the physical part of the job.

The part of the job in which I had absolutely no experience was the administrative work. Prior to taking on the role, I'd never had to learn the seemingly complex business systems required to plan, design and manufacture a race car. I'd never dealt with shipping parts to and from the circuit, creating demand for stock shortages, allocating parts for future events or monitoring mileages in order to schedule their servicing. All of that was new to me and I'd have to master it quickly.

In typical Red Bull fashion, I was thrown in the deep end. By the time I officially took on the role early in 2016, the beginning of the season was already upon us. I would end up getting a few races to shadow a more experienced technician before he retired to factory life, and then my first race on my own would be, of all places, Monaco.

Now, I've made no secret of my general disdain for the week we spend in the principality. It's not that I don't like the place, it's just that it's an absolute nightmare to work in those garages. Tiny, noisy and sweaty, there's really nothing very 'F1' about a week working in the Monaco garages. It certainly wasn't an ideal place to take the reins but, from my perspective, the weekend went without any major hitch. Being thrown in the deep end has always been my favourite way to learn. Unfortunately for the team, the weekend didn't go quite so well, with a communication error resulting in Daniel Ricciardo dropping out of the lead of the race as he sat in the pitlane waiting for his tyres to arrive. That was a lesson we all learned the hard way.

When I got a job at the team that had won four consecutive drivers' and constructors' championships between 2010 and 2013, you could have forgiven me for thinking that it wouldn't be long until I'd get an opportunity to earn that accolade too. What I certainly wasn't expecting was that we would spend the next six years getting our arses kicked by a Mercedes team that, for a time, seemed truly unbeatable. They did everything well. Even though we'd be able to snatch the odd win here and there, take our luck when it came and make the most of the tracks that didn't particularly suit our rivals, each year we'd start the season with so much hope and, by race three, we were pretty much certain that it was a race for second place.

Competing for second isn't what Red Bull is about. We're here to win and all of those years were painful. The worst bit about it all was that, for a large part, it was out of our hands. Red Bull Racing, for most of the last twenty years, have been an engine 'customer', meaning that while they designed and manufactured their own chassis, gearbox and suspension, they bought an engine from another manufacturer and designed the chassis to fit. This is the case for a lot of teams, to varying degrees. Williams have long been supplied an engine by Mercedes and, in some cases, teams even use gearboxes as well as engines supplied by another team, all within the rules of the sport.

Red Bull Racing, from 2007 to 2018, bought engines from Renault. When you're a customer team, being supplied an engine and having to build a car around it, you really are at the supplier's mercy. If that supplier underdelivers, you're fucked. I refer to my time with the Renault V6 as the 'dark days'. Before I tell you what it was like, bear in mind that the opportunity to take the race-team job on so quickly after joining the team only came about because the person in the role prior to me had decided, just one season in, that it wasn't for him. I'm not sure what it was that put him off the job. It might have been the week where six engines failed, one of them on an out lap, or any of the other races that year where the RB11 racing car was plagued with reliability issues. Either way, his loss was my gain, sort of.

Aside from the performance issues of the Renault power unit, the reliability and service requirements to get an engine through a race weekend were appalling. If it wasn't a spark plug, it was a cylinder pressure sensor or one of the many, many other issues. The hours spent stripping down engines on Friday nights to 'service' parts that should comfortably have been able to cover 800 km, the approximate mileage you'd expect in one weekend, were ridiculous.

Although there was a myriad of issues, there were two periods between 2016 and 2018 that were particularly infuriating. The first of these was what I remember as 'Water Pump Gate'. We went through a period where it seemed impossible to get through a race weekend without, at some point, having to change a leaking water pump. To make things worse, there seemed absolutely no logical explanation as to why they were failing. It wasn't like we knew they had the potential to leak after a certain mileage. If that were the case, we could have at least tried to keep to a routine of when we would replace it each weekend. This issue seemed entirely random and, for a long time, there didn't seem to be any plan for how or when the issue might be rectified. For me, any week that I could get through without having to strip an engine apart on a Friday or Saturday night to swap a water pump was a good one.

In one such incident, we'd changed a leaky water pump just prior to qualifying on Saturday. This involved first removing the gearbox in order to then remove the primary exhaust manifold, the heatshields, the hydraulic pump, and then finally the water pump. It was time consuming, and once the car was back together we then had to go through all the hydraulic checks and fire-ups required to get it out on track. Post-qualifying, we'd done all of the usual checks (water pump included, of course) and covered the car up for the night. You can imagine the mood in the garage on Sunday morning when we removed the cover and saw a small puddle of water under the car and drips seeping through the central plank of the floor. So, we did it all again. Floor off, gearbox off . . . we were well versed in the routine by then.

One of the things that makes a car crew fast is routine, and everyone knowing what their jobs are in that process. Guests in the Red Bull garage often comment on how incredible it is to see the work going on like clockwork with the music so loud and nobody really being able to communicate with one another. It's true, there are certain times in the routine of your race weekend where everyone knows the process and you just crank up the music and get on with it.

On this occasion, by the time we'd got the car back together (with its third water pump of the weekend) and started to do the fire-ups before refitting the floor, we were getting pushed for time. So, when we started the engine and almost immediately the brand new pump started leaking, we resorted to truly desperate measures. There was no way that we would have had the time to do the job again and make it to the grid, so we had to find a bodge. We drained as much water from the engine as we could, dried it, and then filled the entire cavity around the water pump of this engine with silicone adhesive. We just took one of the pneumatic silicone guns and unloaded the entire cartridge around the pump. It certainly wasn't pretty, but it worked: the car finished the race.

There was another painful period for me, as the person responsible for dressing and looking after the parts for the eight engines that we had in the garage at one point. This was during the 2018 season, and what I referred to as Renault's weekly game of 'musical turbos', whereby it seemed that each week there would be a sort of turbo lottery to designate which one of the many engines would receive which turbo and MGU-H (which stands for Motor Generator Unit – Heat, the exhaust's heat energy recovery system). We joked that at Renault's Viry-Châtillon factory they had a large tombola and engineers would take turns picking out numbers that would allocate the parts each week. It had to have been completely random because, after many, many years, none of us in the garage could see any logical pattern to it. One week a turbo would have to be swapped out on a spare engine, due to some spurious concern, and then the following week it would be the best one we had and go on a prime engine. Then the next race, it would all change again. It was absolutely ludicrous.

It was all of this that led to the incident where Daniel Ricciardo won the 2018 Chinese Grand Prix with a quarter-inch spanner lodged between the engine and gearbox – a spanner that I had dropped. This had happened while we were frantically swapping an engine after one of the regular failures. It was an insane effort from everyone in the garage to get Daniel out just in time to qualify, start Sunday's race in sixth, and go on to win.

The thing about that incident is that it shouldn't have been that tight to get the car finished in the first place: we'd done so many of these swaps that we were pretty damn quick. The problem was that on Friday evening, just after free practice had concluded, Renault decided that they had to remove the new turbo from Ricciardo's spare engine because it was needed to build another engine . . . at another team. As I said before, you really are at the mercy of the supplier. We'd been assured that another turbo would be available to put on Ricciardo's spare engine first thing the following morning, but as the light at the end of the pitlane went green at the start of FP3 – the third and final free practice session – that turbo was still in a box, with the engine nowhere near being ready to go into a chassis. When Ricciardo's engine almost inevitably failed during that final practice session, the scramble was on.

One of the things that you learn quickly when you're racing is that these things will always happen at the worst possible time. Sometimes it can feel like a collective effort of various different unseen forces have conspired against you. To be perfectly honest, it felt that way most of the time during the 'dark days'. Winning wasn't usually a realistic proposition without something dramatic happening to the cars ahead of us and then, often, when it looked like we might be in a position to win, I'd just be sitting in the garage praying that the engine didn't let us down.

When I dropped that spanner, just prior to qualifying, I wasn't too worried about it. The reason for this was because we were also dealing with an ongoing issue with clutch actuator bearings. This necessitated us removing gearboxes after qualifying each week, with FIA permission, in order to inspect the bearings. In my mind, I was going to get an opportunity to rescue the spanner and check no other damage had been done in just an hour's time when the session ended. After Daniel managed to qualify in sixth, getting out of the garage with around a minute to spare, I told chief mechanic Phil Turner that I'd dropped the spanner. He felt the same way as me, that it would be fine and that we'd sort it later when we removed the gearbox. However, as I said, sometimes it just feels like everything is conspiring against you and, on this particular day, that conspirator was the FIA.

The governing body had grown tired of us requesting permission to inspect the clutch bearings after qualifying every week, and had told the team that unless we could prove that there was an issue, permission was going to be denied. This completely fucked me and my plan to retrieve that spanner.

Speaking to Phil on Sunday morning, just prior to going to the grid, he just said something like, 'Just don't tell Pedals . . .'

As soon as Daniel was leading that race after a fortunately timed safety car allowed us an advantageous pitstop, my anxiety went through the roof. I sat there wondering at what point the small, Snap-on quarter-inch spanner was going to chafe a hole in the exhaust secondary or a heatshield and cause a retirement.

Opportunities to win in 2018 were few and far between and I was certain that if I were to cost us one, I'd be finished! Normally, when you take the chequered flag as the winner, it's supposed to be joyful. That day, it was mostly just relief. It's one of my favourite wins. Although I'd never choose a difficult weekend, there is something to be said for the extra sense of achievement when you do triumph against adversity. Sitting in the bar that night after packing up the circus, it felt like we'd really earned those beers!

I tell young mechanics that they shouldn't be afraid of making mistakes once: it's going to happen. Learning and improving is part of the journey. In this instance, I might not be able to guarantee that I'll never drop anything ever again, but I learned never to allow a situation like that to occur in the first place. Better preparation of spares and contingency plans is something that we've all improved on as a team. In racing, if you allow room for something to go wrong, it will. It's something that Red Bull's sporting director Jonathan Wheatley was constantly reminding those of us in the garage about. If you say to yourself, 'Oh, that'll be fine,' it won't. You might get lucky and just about get away with it, like I did that day in China, but more than likely, you'll learn the hard way.

Despite the struggles with engines in those years, I wouldn't suggest for a minute that the Red Bull team were perfect throughout all of that time. The RB10 in 2014, while actually being quite fast (if you exclude a Mercedes that was in a class of its own), was absolutely awful to build and work on. In the factory, we often refer to it as 'the car that broke Crunch' because No. 1 mechanic Mark 'Crunch' Lenton decided to call time on his racing days at the end of that season.

The RB11 was not only unreliable and hard to work on in 2015, but it was also slow, mostly due to the compromises made on the chassis side to try and claw back losses from the underperforming power unit. When we finished fourth in the constructors' championship that year, the team's worst performance since 2008, I had to wonder if I was just a bad omen. Perhaps I had doomed Marussia and now brought bad karma with me? However, in all the subsequent cars, we seemed to make significant improvements.

The biggest difference between us and our supplier was that, when we had issues with the car, we fixed them and kept moving forwards. We learned from every mistake and we were fast to react to everything. I think that the frustration with Renault's engines came from the lack of progress. I remember one of the Renault technicians telling me during 'Water Pump Gate' that the reason nothing had been done yet was because the designer responsible was off work. I thought he was joking at first. Surely, somebody else just picks up the workload, right?

On top of all that, I still couldn't tell you today who was really in charge at the circuit when it came to the engines. The management structure was just ridiculous. There would be groups of people (all of whom could have been management, who knows?) who used to congregate in the engine-build area during busy build days. Sometimes, it felt like it was on purpose. They'd host these sort of unofficial meetings in French, while standing around with a coffee, leaning on my desk. I'd be squeezing past them, trying to get one of the many engines built an hour before the session started. My French was nowhere near good enough to try and track any of these conversations, so instead I'd just try and judge by the tone and the looks on their faces as to whether the outcome of this meeting was likely to be good or bad news for me. For the most part, the Renault technicians themselves were really good guys and they shared the same frustrations that we had. It seemed that, each week, they took the brunt for things that they had absolutely no control over.

There's really nothing worse than being in a position to win a race against the odds and having a mechanical failure. Engineers and drivers make cars fast. Our job as mechanics is to make a race car safe and reliable. So, no matter the cause of a DNF due to mechanical failure, as a crew, you always take it personally. You bear that responsibility.

At points during the 2018 season, I'd genuinely started to wonder how long I could continue in my role for. The workload was absolutely insane and, each week, I'd arrive at the circuit on a Wednesday morning to be informed of some new and exciting problem that would necessitate me stripping down all of the engines to rectify or check something. Or spending the day playing 'musical turbos' for some reason that nobody seemed to be able to reasonably explain. The situation was so severe that the team, at the behest of Jonathan Wheatley, created the role of 'senior power unit assembly technician' for me as a way of recognising that the work I was having to do was far greater than what was expected of an 'engine kitter'. The role hadn't existed prior to that. Perhaps I should thank Renault: the good that came out of it all was that I got a senior title and a small pay bump.

I was even at the point where I'd started looking at internal vacancies within the team to see if I could find a role that would be a little more palatable. Unfortunately, nobody was looking like they'd vacate any of the roles that I'd want to do on the race team, so I was stuck, unless I wanted to go back to the factory or leave the team, which I didn't.

I remember rationalising to myself that when you think of how many people there are in the paddock, working behind the scenes to achieve the same goal as I was, the chances of being in the right place at the right time to win were actually fairly slim. I considered that I might not be one of the few that do get to call themselves a constructors' champion. I was there to win, and winning was in the DNA of the team, but I don't think I was prepared for how long that road back to glory would take. It was a journey fraught with struggle, disappointment and frustration.

When Red Bull Racing partnered with Honda as its engine supplier for the 2019 season, the tide finally started to turn. Despite Honda's project with McLaren having been fraught with issues, we'd seen the progress that the Japanese marque had made with our sister team, Toro Rosso, the year before, and there was a great sense of confidence around the factory that we would make this new alliance work.

This confidence was further boosted when the new Honda-powered RB15 managed a podium in the opening race of the season in Australia. It was Honda's first podium for eleven years. When we went on to win the Austrian Grand Prix that same year, I saw it as the next milestone in both Red Bull and Honda's return to glory in Formula One. Seeing so many of the Japanese technicians in floods of tears at that podium ceremony was a reminder of just how important it was to all of them. It was as if they were carrying the pride of Japan on their shoulders, and we were all proud to have helped them to achieve this monumental first step on the way to success.

For me, working alongside Honda has been a dream. Their desire to succeed, and willingness to do whatever was required to achieve success, gave me a new lease of energy. I'd go as far as to say that, had the Honda partnership never happened, I don't think I would have stayed in the job for as long as I have. In the garage, the most notable change since switching supplier was the way in which Honda operated. Gone were the days where I'd walk into the engine-build area and trip over a turbo or slip in a puddle of oil that had been spilled and left unattended. During the 'dark days' the engine assembly area often resembled a scrapyard, with bits of power units scattered around the place while the Renault technicians frantically tried to rectify some issue or another. Honda were very disciplined in their operational procedures, tidy, and they double- and triple-checked every bit of work that they did. It was a completely different experience.

During this same period, McLaren had taken on the Renault engine, having grown tired of trying to make it work with Honda, and with Fernando Alonso having quite publicly slated the Japanese manufacturer at every opportunity. I imagined that McLaren were in for quite a shock with Renault. As a team, McLaren have a reputation in the paddock of being very organised and very strict about procedures and cleanliness in the garage, something born out of the Ron Dennis era. We joked that they'd lose their minds when they realised that their floors would now be covered in spilled fluids and walking through the engine area would likely become a treacherous journey through an obstacle course of parts strewn about the place. As a result, I wasn't surprised that the partnership didn't last long before McLaren, quite sensibly, chose to revert back to Mercedes's engine supply.

Over the course of Mercedes's period of domination on the track, Red Bull Racing, as an operation, worked to improve in almost every aspect. Although we knew that we were unable to challenge the Mercedes cars for most of that period, as the Mercedes engines were just too far ahead of the Renault power unit that we were stuck with, we always believed that we were a better team. We did things that other teams seemingly couldn't, like managing to carry out repairs in record time after setbacks. When we managed to get Daniel Ricciardo out for that Chinese GP qualifying session, mechanics from the Renault garage said that they were amazed that we'd managed it and that, in the same circumstances, they would never have been able to get their car out of the door in time. The same can be said for the crew that managed to repair Max Verstappen's car on the grid of the 2020 Hungarian GP. Changing all the left-hand front suspension, after Max had ventured into the wall in mixed conditions on his way to the grid, was an incredible feat that left those who watched on in awe.

Each issue that we overcame – every tough weekend, every failure – made us a better crew in the garage. 'No losses, only lessons' is a phrase I use often. Back in Milton Keynes, the designers in the factory were the most prolific in bringing upgrades that worked to the car each week, and they did so very quickly. We consistently set the benchmark in the pitlane. The engineering and strategy teams also shone throughout those years, constantly putting us in a position to pick up any wins possible and capitalise on even the smallest of errors from our competitors. We worked tirelessly to ensure that when the opportunity to mount a serious title challenge did appear, we were ready for it.

Reliability, ease of build and how we managed servicing work were now all in our own hands. The new partnership with Honda was a part of that improvement but, in addition, we focused on things like pitstop performance, manufacturing, parts management and logistics. We knew that in order to topple the mighty Mercedes, all of these things would have to come together.

Entering the 2021 season with a car that clearly had the potential to be a world championship winner, and Max Verstappen in the kind of form required to be a world champion, we knew from the off that this was the year when we could seriously consider that the title drought might come to an end.

*

The 2021 Formula One World Championship was the toughest year of my professional life. The workload alone was immense. While this is true every year, the mounting pressure throughout that season, and knowing that any mistake made in the garage would likely spell the end of our championship hopes, raised the stress to a whole new level. As the advantage in both the constructors' and drivers' championships swung to-and-fro, each race that passed raised the intensity.

It was certainly the first time that the job really took its toll on my mental health. Not only was the time at the circuit incredibly stressful but switching off afterwards became almost impossible towards the end of the season. It felt as though we were prey being hunted.

Earlier in the year, it had looked as if we would win the championship comfortably, but as the development race seemed to swing in our opponents' favour towards the end of the season, it looked as if the chance was slipping away with each passing race.

If you embark on a career in racing, you're going to have some pretty rough days at work from time to time. Things will go wrong with the car, you'll make mistakes, and you'll even fall out with close colleagues. It's stressful. I always advise people to try to separate the days when things get tough. When the garage door closes each evening and you leave the circuit, that's it, it's done, tomorrow we go again. That wasn't the case at all toward the back end of 2021.

When I'd fly home after a race looking forward to some rest, it just never came. Before I knew it, I'd be back on a coach headed for Heathrow carrying the stresses of the previous races with me. When I was home, I was hardly present at all. I had no energy. Phoebe's patience with me was incredible. My mental health was really suffering. I was pretty miserable at the circuit and I was struggling to get out of my own head when at home. This all culminated in me ending up having a bit of a 'what the fuck am I doing here?' moment in Qatar that year, a bit of a meltdown.

It was the last stint of a gruelling triple-header, and we'd flown (for over fifteen hours) from Brazil. We were all exhausted. I woke up on the Friday morning prepared for a typically stressful first day on track, and while getting ready in the plush room of the St Regis hotel, I put on *30*, the newly released Adele album. Before I knew it, while brushing my teeth and hearing 'My Little Love' for the first time, I just broke down. I was physically and mentally exhausted, jet-lagged, and I missed my daughter, Isabella. Here I was, a grown man, standing in the bathroom holding his toothbrush and crying his eyes out.

The reason I tell you all this is because what happened next speaks to what it's like to be a part of my team. I imagine most people in my state that morning would have just tried to tidy themselves up and get through the day quietly. If you don't feel supported in the environment that you're in, then that's pretty much the only option. There's not a great deal of mental health support for full-time travelling staff in the paddock and, while that's improving, you really have to rely on your teammates. Rather than keep it all to myself, I got ready (feeling like shit) and in the van I spoke to the car crew. I told them that I'd just had a little meltdown (and jokingly advised against listening to the Adele album until we were home). During the drive to the circuit, we talked about the stresses we were all under and, although I was still missing home, by the time we'd arrived I was ready to crack on and get it done.

Within the team, physio John Hammond had become the unofficial mental health support, the person to whom lots of people spoke about the personal issues they were dealing with. John sort of unwillingly fell into this role as the team's agony aunt. It's understandable really. It sort of makes sense that while John was helping to relieve a physical ailment, people would use him to share what had been on their mind too. I would lean on John plenty during the regular treatments my back required throughout the year.

With regard to getting through the 2021 season, there was no real answer on how I dealt with the stress. I told myself that, quite simply, there were two choices. Either I could put the issues to the back of my mind and get on with the job in hand without worrying about the eventual outcome of the season. Or I could quit, tell the team that I couldn't deal with it all any more, request that I be moved into a factory-based role for the remainder of the season, and rob myself of the potential glory that I'd been working towards for the last decade. The choice was simple. I had to move forward.

I relied on those in the garage in the same position as me to prop me up when I needed it, and I ensured that I was there to do the same for them. Being close with my teammates was crucial.

To work for Red Bull Racing is different from every other outfit in the sport. When the team entered F1 in 2005, it was clear from the outset that they were going to do things differently, and that same mindset is true today. They've never tried to replicate what their competitors are doing. Rather, it's always been about finding a different way to win. When guests of the garage comment on just how organised and well-oiled we look as a team, I usually think to myself, *Really?* To me, it often feels like chaos, but it's a chaos that we're comfortable with. I've always said that Red Bull Racing are exactly what Enzo Ferrari would have described as 'garagistas'. I like to refer to us as the 'pitlane pirates'.

I suppose the way that I'd summarise the top teams in Formula One is to say that Ferrari are about history and heritage, Mercedes are about process and procedure, and Red Bull are all about the people. There's not really a better way to describe how the teams differ in their approach to the sport.

In 2014, I would have jumped at absolutely any opportunity to stay in the paddock. Whoever made me the first offer, I would have given 100 per cent to them. If you're an aspiring motorsport mechanic or engineer, you should do exactly the same. That I happened to land at Red Bull almost seems like it was destiny. As a guy that's stubborn, persistent and hates conformity, it was lucky that I found a team whose ethos was to 'win differently', and do whatever it takes to do so. Moreover, a team that considered the people it employs, and what they bring to the table, as its greatest asset was exactly what I needed. I can't say that I knew all of this when I took the job, but I learned it very quickly.

One thing that all new starters at the team will tell you is how welcoming the place is and how quickly you'll feel at home. It's hard for a massive company to feel so personal. Somehow Red Bull manage that despite having close to two thousand people on the campus. Admittedly, this is probably truer for those of us who travel together, as with all of the crews on the grid, but for Red Bull Racing it's part of a wider philosophy to put faith in people over process. Now, in my role at the circuit, I never feel micromanaged. Those I report to know that I'll get it done without interference and I'll communicate effectively throughout the business to overcome any hurdles. What I do with my workday isn't logged beyond the total 'F1-related' hours I do each day, which is only a requirement due to the cost cap. Beyond that, I'm pretty much left to get on with it. This is true throughout most of the team.

We have faith in each other to deliver for one another and it works. It works so well that it's created a very unified team. This style of management is so effective at creating a cohesive unit and making employees feel valued that, prior to the cost cap, staff retention on the race team was incredibly high. This was despite the long hours and stresses of the job. Those that did leave usually did so just because they wanted to stop travelling, and it was very rare for people to jump ship to other teams in the same paddock.

It's a philosophy that only works if you hire the right people for the right jobs, and it's not just about technical skill. As a unit, the race team at Red Bull Racing is a prime example of 'soft skills' being taken into account as a key factor when considering who is the best candidate for a high-stress job.

The decisions on which mechanics at the team would progress to being trackside ultimately fell to Jonathan Wheatley, and was an area in which he excelled. Although it's been a long time since Jonathan was 'in the field' as a mechanic, he understood the dynamic in the garage, he knew the environment, and he was excellent at judging whether a personality was going to 'work' in that environment. He also knew what made people tick, and how to get the best out of them.

'Soft skills' was a concept that I saw excellently explained to a school group in Milton Keynes by radio

DJ Alex Mansuroglu. We both participated in a BBC Bitesize careers day at a school in 2023, and Alex asked the group of kids to picture their current friend groups. He explained that in every friend group you have the organiser, the joker, the person who keeps everyone safe and the confident leader. It was a great way to highlight to young people that they already have some of the skills they'll need in the workplace; they're already part of their personalities.

All of these 'soft skills' are crucial to a race team and these personality traits are things that are crucial to managers hiring for travelling roles in motorsport. For Red Bull Racing, these are some of the most important skills that you need to showcase to be considered for travelling roles.

The characters that Jonathan Wheatley assembled on the race team at Red Bull undoubtedly play a large part in the team's success. Everyone has a role to play in the team – an unofficial role beyond their job description. These characters are the foundation of the very different atmosphere you'll find in our garage. For starters, the team is full of instigators. Whenever some sort of 'sketch' is going on – an elaborate practical joke, fabricated rumour or just something childishly humorous – there's a fairly long list of people that you'd immediately expect to be responsible for it. For a group of highly skilled and driven individuals, you'd be amazed at how much time and effort some find to pour into practical jokes and clownish behaviour.

The list of practical jokes is endless but there are a few that been highlights over the years. One of my personal favourites was always when someone managed to slowly fill a colleague's rucksack with small bits of ballast throughout the week, each day adding a little more so that the extra weight went unnoticed until Sunday night, when the victim would go to pack for the flight home and discover that they'd been carrying around an extra kilo of Densamet tungsten.

I discovered quite early on that some people were far too skilled and dangerous to play practical jokes on. Usually these were older members of the team, or those who'd previously served in the armed forces. These racing veterans who had seen it all, and knew far too many ways to make your life a misery, were always best left alone. It really wasn't worth it; you'd always lose in the end. There really is no replacement for experience.

One of the people that I always steered clear of messing with was gearbox technician Andrew Davies, affectionately known in the paddock as 'Mavis'. Mavis was a master of practical jokes, as he'd had plenty of practice during his time with the Royal Air Force. Electronics technician Adam Wootton learned this the hard way once after loudly bragging in front of Mavis that he didn't have to stay on at work to cover an in-season test. The moment Adam departed to return home, Mavis got to work. After locating the tray of tools that Adam used to work around the car, Mavis painstakingly wrapped every single tool in the tray in packing tape. Even down to the small 2-mm Allen keys: every single tool got wrapped individually. That might seem mildly inconvenient on its own, but what Mavis did next was diabolical. He sprayed the entire set of newly wrapped tools with WD-40. This, of course, made it all very slippery. It was now nearly impossible to find the end of each piece of tape and peel it off.

So, when Adam got to the circuit on the Wednesday of the following race, he discovered that before he was able to do any work, he'd have to spend the next hour or so 'unpacking' his tools, much to the amusement of all of us. I can't imagine how sore the ends of his fingers got, trying to grip the ends of the slippery plastic tape and peel it off from around a hundred individual tools.

In another incident, hydraulics technician Tom Miles and I had been lucky enough not to have to cover a post-race filming day in Budapest. Instead of staying to run the car, we had the privilege of a 'Hollywood' flight home as soon as the flag dropped after the race on Sunday. This had already annoyed Mavis and then, to make it worse, Tom had spent the week winding him up about it.

As we were leaving straight after the race, Tom and I had brought our travel clothes with us to the circuit on Sunday morning. Tom made the mistake of leaving his set hanging up in the truck, so Mavis, once again, hatched a brilliant plan. Tucked away at the Hungaroring, there's a decent shower and changing room under the garages at the far end of the paddock. So, Tom and I had decided that we'd grab a quick shower and change when the race finished, before hopping in the airport transfer and disappearing off home. It seemed a decent plan – feel nice and fresh for the flight home, a nice treat as we headed into the summer break.

Post-shower, I was just getting dressed when from the other side of the changing room I heard Tom suddenly shout, 'Fucking Mavis!'

I knew that whatever Mavis had done was going to be good. When Tom had attempted to fasten the buttons on his travel shirt, they had all popped off in his hands one by one. He had got to the third or fourth button before realising that he'd been a victim of Mavis's hijinks. In his usual remorseless fashion, Mavis had very carefully taken a scalpel to Tom's shirt and cut all but a single thread on the buttons, so they looked fine when the shirt was still hanging up. Mavis had left just the very top and the very bottom buttons, so Tom had to walk back down the busy paddock trying to hold his shirt together with his stomach on show. It was so simple, but so ridiculously inconvenient I nearly pissed myself. Tom ended up having to use double-sided tape to keep his shirt closed for our journey home. So much for a Hollywood exit.

Among the technicians, this kind of thing is constant. Small, odd, inconvenient little things like supergluing someone's mouse to their desk. Superglue was in action again at a test in 2023 when one of the garage technicians managed to stick a gearbox tech's shoe to the ground with glue and activator . . . while he was standing in them, working on the car. He managed to glue them so well, in fact, that when the gearbox technician eventually went to walk away from the job he was doing, he ripped the shoe clean in half, then had to chisel the sole off of the middle of the garage floor.

I think that the technicians, as most of our work is around the back of the garage, tend to find more time for this kind of thing, and it helps to relieve the stress. I once filled all of Tom's empty damper travel bags with bananas halfway through the season. Tom thought that he'd found and removed them all at the following race, but when we arrived in Abu Dhabi at the end of that year, the putrid smell and the colony of flies coming from his storage cabinet suggested otherwise. Needless to say, Tom wasn't best pleased to find the new ecosystem that had taken over one of the drawers.

Nobody is spared this kind of thing in the Red Bull garage. If you create an opportunity for people to mess with you, somebody is going to take it. Even the drivers like to get in on it. When Paul, a rear-end mechanic with a reputation for being particularly sleepy, decided to take an extended nap in the lounge of Hong Kong airport, Daniel Ricciardo took it upon himself to treat him to a new face tattoo with a permanent marker. Paul only began to realise that something was up when people's uncontrollable laughter, as he boarded the plane, raised his suspicions. When he was shown a picture of the gang-affiliated 'teardrop' tattoo down the side of his face, he was hilariously furious.

Even Jonathan Wheatley wasn't spared the madness. On one occasion during a test session, Jonathan made the mistake of leaving his laptop open in the engineering office when he went to sit on the pit wall. This laptop was set up to screen share with his monitor on the pit wall and as the cars were going round the circuit, a horrified Jonathan realised that one of his screens was now playing pornography for the whole pitlane to see. One of the drivers had seen his open laptop and seized an opportunity to fuck with him.

Even though he'd walk around the garage in his stern and authoritative manner, I think Jonathan quite enjoyed it when people included him in the garage banter – it helped him feel like one of the boys and reminded him of his origins in the sport.

As much as this kind of behaviour can be inconvenient and frustrating at the time (when it happens to you), I genuinely wouldn't have it any other way. I just couldn't imagine surviving twenty-four races a year in some stale, entirely professional environment where everyone was just helpful and pleasant to one another all day. How boring. I couldn't do it.

People often ask me if I'd ever go and work for another F1 team. As I've said previously, I never ignore an opportunity. Also, there are plenty of other great teams to work for in the paddock. Mercedes is an incredibly well-managed organisation, their employee benefits are great and they earn more than us. The latter of those also applies to McLaren, who have traditionally had the highest earning mechanics in the pitlane. Ferrari's passion and sense of family stands out in the paddock, even if carrying the dreams of the Tifosi comes with inherent added pressure. More recently, we've started to see quite a few people – including Jonathan Wheatley, who has been with Red Bull Racing since 2006 – head over to Sauber in Switzerland, in anticipation of Audi's entry in 2026. The draw of minimising one's tax bill is understandably enticing. Each team has its benefits, but most importantly for anyone wishing to get into the sport, it's crucial to take any opportunity to get into the paddock.

The truth is, had any other team made me an offer prior to Red Bull, although I would have jumped at it, there has to be a question mark over how long I would have lasted. I'm opinionated and outspoken, and not particularly good at 'staying in my lane'. To be honest, there's not many places that would have tolerated me for as long as Red Bull have. Part of the 'win differently' mentality inherently entails a general disregard for process or tradition in favour of results, and that's me all over. I don't care how I get to where I'm going. If the path less trodden is the quickest route, bring it on. Me joining Red Bull Racing was a case of two attitudes in harmony.

One thing that I know for certain is that no other team in the paddock would have allowed me to build a large social media following, to the point where I became a sort of unofficial ambassador for the team, and then, with no supervision, go off and do interviews, podcasts and write this book. While there were some who were unhappy about me doing all that, nobody really put much effort into curbing it. Pretty much any of that activity would have seen me in an HR office fairly quickly at another team. From what I hear from friends of mine up and down the paddock, it's likely that my distain for process and hierarchy would have landed me in a fair amount of hot water too. Ultimately, I think I landed exactly where I needed to be. So, while it's absolute chaos at times, I don't think I would want to do the same job anywhere else.

The 2021 championship battle was like the opening showcase of the work that we'd been doing behind the scenes to improve as an operation for the last seven years. We made no tangible mistakes as a unit in the garage that year. The car was fast and reliable, Max showcased his once-in-a-generation talent, the strategies worked out and the pit crew consistently set the benchmark for pitstop performance. We were pretty much flawless in the garage in one of the toughest seasons the sport has ever seen.

I think we can all agree that without a fair chunk of bad luck in races like Baku and Hungary, the championship wouldn't have come down to a last-race showdown at all. But that's racing: sometimes things go your way, sometimes they don't. Despite how people may feel about the controversy that shadowed the outcome of Abu Dhabi 2021 – with Max pipping Lewis after the safety car episode – nothing will ever detract from the work put in by everyone involved in that season's championship fight in both the Red Bull and Mercedes garages. It was an incredible effort.

That season was the beginning of something very special at Red Bull. With the momentum off the back of Max's first drivers' championship and a new opportunity in the form of a drastic technical regulations change, we all went in to 2022 full of confidence. It wasn't the easiest start to the season; we had a double DNF in Bahrain, and then a further retirement in Australia a few weeks later. While we knew that we were fast, we understood that those kind of failures or mistakes cost championships. But, in typical fashion, we brushed them off and got back to work.

From that point on, the momentum just seemed to grow and grow. With both of our drivers – Sergio Pérez alongside Max – delivering solid results week in, week out, and the car running almost perfectly (no race car is perfect; every week there's something that needs monitoring or special attention), we spent the rest of the first half of the season applying pressure on our rivals Ferrari, fairly confident that we'd win out.

Winning the constructors' championship in 2022, the team's first since 2013 and my very first, meant that I'd finally achieved that last elusive goal that I'd set myself. I joked with Jonathan Wheatley that I could retire now and do something easier. He immediately responded, 'You'll always want another one.' He was right. It's addictive, winning, especially after so many years of falling short.

What made 2022 even better was that the company's race bonus scheme covered the top three places, so while we wanted to win every week, as long as we put the car on the podium, it paid out. This proved so lucrative for us (and costly for the team) that, for the 2023 season, the bonus scheme changed to only paying out if we won. We were victims of our own success.

In 2023, however, it didn't matter. By this point our momentum was unstoppable. With the design office having got the car right from the beginning of this set of regulations and continuing to build from there, we went on to have the most successful season ever in Formula One, winning twenty-one of the twenty-two races and showing no signs of slowing down. Each time a technical directive was issued that our competitors hoped would slow us down, Max went faster. It was an incredible year. The RB19 was the best car ever produced on the Milton Keynes campus and being a part of the team that made that season happen is one of my proudest achievements. Even so, I'm still annoyed that we couldn't make it work in Singapore – perfection was so close!

It's hard to predict where the team will stand with the next big rule change in 2026. An overhaul of the engine regulations and some fairly drastic changes to the aero regulations, including the potential for 'active' aerodynamic assemblies such as electronically controlled front wing flaps, will present a host of new challenges for all of the teams. For Red Bull Racing, producing a new engine, the first manufactured in-house by Red Bull Powertrains, will make 2026 a defining year for the team. Just as we've seen at the start of every new era in the sport, the introduction of new regulations always presents new opportunities, but for Red Bull, 2026 also poses a huge amount of risk. In terms of the new engines, it is very much a trip into the unknown for the team. As a company that has never mass-produced an engine for race or road use previously, to take on the challenge of building the team's first in-house designed and manufactured Formula One power unit is hugely ambitious. I'm sure there are plenty, including myself, who are intrigued about how it will perform.

The teams' detractors will, no doubt, be hoping that the project is an abject failure. It is worth noting, though, that these same people would have laughed back in 2005 if you had told them that Red Bull Racing would go on to change the sport, defeat all the established racing powerhouses and break records. Thankfully, the team are no strangers to underdog status and when they go up against Mercedes, Ferrari, the newly joining Audi and current partners Honda, that's certainly what Red Bull Powertrains will be. It's highly unlikely that it's going to be smooth sailing. It will be a steep learning curve with plenty of lessons learned the hard way. However, in my view, if there's ever been a team that could take on something so far from their comfort zone and ultimately come out on top, it's Red Bull.

CHAPTER 6

On the Road

In my role as senior power unit assembly technician, I'm ultimately responsible for the assembly of all the parts and systems that integrate an engine into our chassis. This includes all of the pipework, heatshields, coolers and exhaust systems. My job is to ensure that, for each event, all the required engines are prepared to the correct specification, that all the parts fitted are serviced and in good working order, and that engines are available for the mechanics to fit to the car when they are required. I also have to plan for future builds, working ahead of time to ensure that parts are shipped back and forth to the factory in Milton Keynes for service when required. This means that my role is split, about fifty–fifty, between physical labour and administrative work. As with most things in the garage, the physical workload is spread among a few of us. The 'fourth mechanic' is usually the one that takes on the role of assisting with engine-related work alongside the No. 1 mechanic on each car crew. It's a collaborative effort.

In a typical working week at a circuit, we'll arrive on the Wednesday in the F1 paddock of whatever country we're racing in that weekend. Wednesdays are usually one of the busiest days at the circuit for the crews in the garages. It's the day where the mechanics take on the bulk of the work required to build the car. At a 'fly-away' race, where the cars and equipment have arrived at the circuit by air freight, the goal on a Wednesday is essentially to get the cars in one piece. The chassis, gearbox and engines will have all been shipped separately, so the first thing to do is unpack the remainder of the freight, get the garage ready to work in, and then assemble the car to whatever specification has been designated for the weekend, a decision driven by the simulations from various engineering groups in the factory.

The hours that can be worked over the course of a race weekend are restricted by curfew periods that come into force from Wednesday evening and apply to all operational personnel. In addition, teams are not allowed to fire-up engines for the first time until an FIA-designated time on Thursday. The goal by the end of Wednesday is to ensure that all other systems are signed-off in preparation for that first fire-up. Hydraulic and fuel systems, brake logging and gearbox checks all need to be performed prior to firing up the cars, so we always aim to have all of these things done by the end of play, so that, come Thursday, the crew can use the morning to focus on 'setting up' the car.

The entirety of Thursday morning is spent measuring suspension geometry and making any changes required to ensure that things like ride height, wheel camber and a host of other spring and damper adjustments match the race engineers' desired set-up. This baseline, the engineer and drivers' starting point for the weekend, is vitally important. As such, this is now done with some rather expensive but incredibly accurate equipment.

When I started in Formula One, and even when I first joined Red Bull in 2015, set-up was done using simple digital levels, pieces of string and rulers. It was a quick and simple way to measure the geometry but – not surprisingly – it wasn't particularly accurate. About six years ago, Red Bull Racing decided to introduce a Leica Absolute laser tracker into the garage, and use it to set up the car. With the ability to measure components to within 50 microns, or 0.05 millimetres, Leica quickly became a key part of our set-up process. It's an incredible piece of equipment and the software has so many applications throughout the engineering sector that, thinking about it now, it's amazing that we didn't start using it sooner.

It was such an improvement in accuracy when measuring the geometry of the car that, a little while later, the FIA decided to introduce Leica scanning as a way to measure the legality of each component, and it then became mandatory for all teams to use it. Now, all teams have to scan the entire car at the beginning of the season, or whenever they make a significant change to the chassis or bodywork, and provide the FIA with a 'blueprint' of each team's design. This allows the FIA to quickly check if a car is non-compliant at any point during an event and, at random points throughout the season, usually post-qualifying, each car will be summoned to the FIA garage for a 'full scan'. Any of the relevant aerodynamic surfaces, the front and rear wings, the floor and all of the other dimensions defined by the technical regulations can be chosen by the FIA delegates for inspection.

While Leica Absolute is an incredible tool for the team to be able to utilise to improve performance, the drawback is time. Leica scanning takes a tremendous amount of time and dominates most of the workload on a Thursday at the circuit. For a mechanic, if you are unfortunate enough to have your Saturday evening ruined by an FIA car scan, you just pray it isn't at a race somewhere fun such as Montreal or Texas, somewhere that you'd definitely have plans for a night out. If you had to do a late night somewhere like Saudi Arabia or Austria, it wasn't the end of the world.

As the ability to do more with Leica has grown over the years, naturally, the desire to use all of the available tools as often as possible has also grown. Now, it's not just suspension geometry, but also wings, floors and complete three-dimensional models of aero surfaces that we spend most of every Thursday scanning. It takes forever, and the entire time the car is being scanned, you can't touch it or cross the laser while the measuring wizardry is being carried out. This, of course, holds up any other work that needs doing. We often joke with chief engineer Paul Monaghan that Leica is his only friend, a badge he wears with stoic pride.

Once the scanning has all been completed, and the cars have been fired up and signed off, the final part of Thursday's schedule is pitstop practice. It tends to be the longest practice of the week, where the crew will run through all of the different scenarios we may face during the Grand Prix. Nose changes, punctures and penalty stops as well as individual car-crew stops are all the different things we'll go through as we begin our pitlane preparations for the week.

In an ideal world, and with no parts delays or other setbacks, the mechanics leave the circuit prior to the Thursday curfew period with the car complete and ready to run in FP1 on Friday morning. All that's left to do is to plug in the water heater and pop the cover on for the night.

As with everything Red Bull Racing, it's rarely that simple. It's not uncommon for us to be waiting for a wing or even an entire floor or set of bodywork on a Friday morning. With the production and logistics departments aiming to give the design office as much time as possible to bring upgraded parts to the track, we've often pushed the boundaries for shipping parts and having them arrive in time. When we've really pushed the limits, it leaves everyone in the garage scrambling around in a typically chaotic, yet somehow oddly in-control fashion, trying to complete jobs prior to that FP1 on a Friday morning. Jobs that should have been done on Thursday.

In a tale from before my time, after delays getting an upgraded front wing to a circuit for Sebastian Vettel, the team elected to hire a jet and send the wing unfinished. It was then apparently painted mid-flight in the jet, destroying the interior decor of the plane and costing a significant sum to rectify. 'That's so Red Bull' is something I've said hundreds of times over the last ten years, as finding a limit and pushing past it is the norm.

Fridays see the start of the on-track running for the cars. For us in the garage, it's a busy day, usually around twelve hours in the garage re-prepping the cars between sessions, carrying out changes and, of course, more pitstop practice. With the calendar now consisting of twenty-four races, the governing body have imposed even longer curfew periods throughout the race week. This mandatory curfew aims to manage the fatigue for operational personnel by enforcing around twelve hours away from the racetrack. For a European race like Austria, the allowed working period tends to begin at 9.30 a.m. and ends at 10 p.m., with personnel not allowed to return to work until 9.30 a.m. the following day.

Curfew periods in Formula One were first introduced in 2011, but in my first years of the sport, they were much shorter. Fridays used to be absolutely brutal, by far the hardest day of the working week. We used to leave the hotel at 7 a.m. and find ourselves working until curfew at around 1 a.m. You'd then be back at it the following morning.

In the time between the end of FP2 and the end of the day, you'd have an enormous workload. Back then, it was still common for most teams to run a Friday-only engine and gearbox, with them both being replaced for the allocated race engine and box prior to qualifying on Saturday. This meant that as soon as the cars returned to the garage after the final Friday practice session, we would immediately delve into the task of removing all of the bodywork, the floor, the gearbox and then the engine, before refitting the new parts, and redoing in just a few hours all the sign-off processes and set-up work that we'd spent the whole of Thursday doing.

This was also before Leica scanning could be done in your own garage with your own equipment, so all the teams used to also have to then take their cars to the FIA garage and measure their wings and weigh the cars using the FIA weighbridge. Each team was allowed to be on the weighbridge for ten minutes on the Friday evening, but it was first come, first served. Sometimes all the other work fitted in perfectly and you'd be ready to go down to the FIA garage when there was maybe only one other car queuing to use the weighbridge. Other times, you'd push the car out the garage on its skates and see five cars queuing. Just like that, an hour of the evening was gone.

I used to dread those Fridays. Getting through them was like summiting a mountain each week. I'd tell myself that once I'd made it through Friday, it was pretty much downhill from then onwards. With the new, longer curfews and shorter practice sessions (sixty minutes each compared to the previous ninety), Fridays are far more manageable now.

Sprint weekends – there were six of them in 2024 – have been a controversial addition to the Formula One calendar over the last few years, with fans seemingly split over whether they are a welcome change to the traditional schedule of three practice sessions, qualifying on a Saturday afternoon, and then the Grand Prix on Sunday. Now, on Sprint weekends, the additional Sprint qualifying takes place on the Friday with the Sprint itself on the Saturday.

In my role, there are actually some benefits to the Sprint weekend. With the removal of two of the practice sessions and an extra 'parc fermé' period, where the cars can only have certain designated service work carried out on them, Sprint weekends can, depending on the format, ease the workload on the mechanics in the garage.

However, I have to say, I'm not particularly a fan of the Sprint weekends. It's not that I'm averse to change because I'm some sort of traditionalist. I just think that they take something away from a Sunday Grand Prix. Having been to the grid and gone through the pre-race routine already on a Saturday, I always feel that the grid proceedings on a Sunday during a Sprint weekend are a little lacklustre. I never get the same buzz while I'm standing on the grid on Sunday when we've done it all once that weekend already. I'd much prefer that for the Sprint, we got rid of pre-race grid proceedings entirely. I'd prefer it if, for the Sprint, the cars simply filed out of their garages and into the pitlane in the order that they qualified, did a single formation lap to the grid, and went racing, saving the excitement and pre-race grid build-up for Sundays.

As a mechanic, Saturdays are probably my favourite and, as a racing fan, I like a good qualifying session. Completely coincidently, Saturday is also probably the easiest day at the circuit in terms of workload. As the cars are in 'parc fermé' from the moment they roll out of the pitlane for qualifying, meaning no changes or repair work can be carried out without express permission from the FIA, Saturdays often present the best opportunity to go and have a night out.

While Jonathan Wheatley often tried to deter people from going out on a Saturday night in his regular post-qualifying meeting in the garage, I can assure you that the words fell on entirely deaf ears. Try telling a group of twenty- to thirty-year-olds that they'd better not go out and enjoy the nightlife in Budapest, Miami or Austin. It doesn't work.

During the 2021 season, after one of Jonathan's stern post-qualifying garage meetings, one electronics technician was found asleep in a ninth-floor corridor of the Omni hotel in Austin by the head of logistics on Sunday morning.

Thankfully, despite this kind of thing happening regularly, everyone always managed to get the job done. If you fucked up and then Jonathan found out that you'd been out on the piss the night before, your hangover was going to be the least of your worries. But provided you got it done on a Sunday, what's there to complain about?

Back when I was at Marussia, things had not always gone as smoothly when people decided to have a big night out. In Monaco one year, a controls engineer had decided to let his hair down on the Saturday night. At some point in the evening, he knew that he wasn't going to make it back to the hotel in Menton prior to our Sunday morning leaving time, so while he still had the wherewithal to do so, he'd asked others to go into his room, grab some team kit and bring it to the circuit for him. A couple of hours prior to the race, he wasn't looking great. Pale and sweaty, he sat at his desk stinking of alcohol, and his worsening appearance made the extent of his hangover obvious to everyone. But he still seemed to be holding it together. It was all going just fine right up until the final few moments on the grid, just before the formation lap, when the car wouldn't fire up. It turned out that things weren't fine at all and the controls engineer, in his drunken stupor, had forgotten to charge one of the batteries in the cockpit of the car. The car had to be pushed off the grid and into the pitlane. It was a lesson learned the hard way, and I can only imagine that he really did learn it: he went on to win multiple Le Mans after his time in F1.

One of my favourite tales from my time travelling came on the Saturday afternoon of the 2019 Japanese GP, when Saturday running had been cancelled due to the incoming threat of Typhoon Hagibis. It's rare for us to get that kind of free time during a race weekend, so despite the passing typhoon and weather that came with it, a few of us decided to make the most of the time away from the circuit. We did this by doing what we often did with unexpected hours away from the racetrack: we found a bar.

Where we were staying in Yokkaichi, about a half-an-hour drive from Suzuka Circuit, most of the businesses in the town had shut their doors in preparation for the worsening weather. Fortunately for us, one of the only places that was still open was a tiny little bar, commonly referred to as 'Al's Bar' and a popular haunt for paddock personnel. When I say that this bar is tiny, I really mean it. On the corner of the block, it has only one table and four stools. On a busy Sunday night, people would spill out into the street because, as well as cheap Asahi, this tiny bar also served some of the best fried chicken, ramen and gyoza you'll find anywhere.

On this particular Saturday afternoon, with the rain hammering down, Al's Bar was understandably quiet. We were the only people in there and the owner, 'Al', greeted us with his usual smile plus some Japanese words that we didn't understand. We must have been there for about an hour, and were a couple of beers in, when the owner suddenly and rather frantically ushered us off the only table and asked us to move on to the few stools that lined the bar. He then started wiping down the table that we had been sitting at. We thought that he was probably closing due to the weather and he just wanted to square up the place.

As we were discussing where we might go when this place closed, four large black SUVs pulled up outside the bar and four suited men got out and, using umbrellas, made a shelter from the rain between the bar and rear door of one of the cars. While this was happening, Al had pulled an expensive-looking bottle of whisky and a crystal glass out from behind the bar and put them on the table that we had previously been occupying. Then, a large man in a very well-tailored and visibly expensive pinstripe suit emerged from the SUV. As he entered the bar, we all noticed the diamond-encrusted Audemars Piguet watch on his wrist. As the man sat down, Al bowed deeply, greeted him, and then poured a glass of whisky. We all sort of sat there in silence for a minute, not really knowing what to make of it all.

A little while later, the man gestured to Al and he soon appeared with a round of beer for all of us in the bar. We all looked over to the man, gestured with our glasses and said 'Kanpai'. At this point, we noticed that the four men who had previously built an umbrella shelter were now standing in a row, shoulder to shoulder, in the rain. It was clear that their intention was to obscure any view of the bar from the street. And then I noticed that all four of these men were missing the lower part of their little fingers on one hand.

The man seemed like a nice enough guy, and at least he had bought us a round. He didn't stay long, and soon the men in suits who were standing outside, now soaked through from the rain, got their umbrellas back out to make a dry path for their boss. Just as quickly as they'd pulled up, they were gone. Al gestured to us that we could now return to the table. It was all a bit surreal.

I recounted this story the following morning to Yoshino-san, the Honda chief mechanic. Throughout my retelling of the encounter, Yoshi wore his usual intrigued expression. He was smiling all the way up until I mentioned the men's fingers. As soon as I told him this, his expression changed entirely and he immediately said, 'Oh Calum-san, he was yakuza – very dangerous!'

It turned out that we had spent our afternoon off raising a glass with some sort of royalty of the local criminal underworld.

Racing has afforded me an incredible life, full of experiences that few get to enjoy. I try not to take it for granted. Even on the toughest days, I try to remind myself how fortunate I am to have found something from which I love to earn a living.

Even now, with the extended curfew periods, the average working week for an F1 mechanic tends to be in the region of between seventy and eighty hours. The longest of these is normally Sunday, race day.

After my usual big breakfast on a Sunday morning, I head into the garage to take on all of the routine pre-race tasks that have to be completed. Fire-up and pre-flight checks, filling of fluid systems and any outstanding post-qualifying jobs are first on the agenda. After that, I usually have a couple of hours where I can carry out any preparation work for the next event and do any outstanding admin work required to manage the servicing of the car when the race finishes. I usually have a long list of items to check and electronically transact so that parts can be physically stripped and returned to the factory for service post-event.

After that, about an hour prior to the pitlane opening for the cars to make their way to grid, we have our final pitstop practice. It's the last real opportunity the crew get to iron out any kinks and get ourselves into the right mindset to perform under pressure in the race.

Shortly before the cars arrive on the grid, I head out with a couple of my teammates to set up our equipment in the grid slot and prepare to receive the car with cooling fans as it arrives. The half an hour that we spend on the grid, complete with a performance of the national anthem of the country that we're racing in and VIP guests bustling to get a better, up-close glimpse of the cars, is the time that I use to focus and mentally prepare for the race. In some places, the grid is so busy that it's a real challenge to block out all of the noise and distractions and just focus on the task at hand. I treat it almost like a mental warm-up. It's the time I use to get 'in the zone', soaking up the atmosphere and finding the energy required to perform as well as I know I can in the pitlane. The adrenaline of pitstops and the anticipation of that 'fifteen seconds' call dominate the next two hours; we're all focused and ready for anything. When the lights go out, there's no longer anything those of us in the garage can do to influence what happens on track, except for those couple of seconds (hopefully) when the car is being serviced in the pitlane.

Long after the chequered flag has dropped and the fans have headed home, you'll find an army of mechanics and technicians marching cars and equipment around the paddock. It's quite a chaotic time in the paddock, and you'll always hear music thumping out of the Red Bull garage. Whether we're using air freight or trucks to transport the equipment, the pack-up operation will go on late into the night and will then be continued on the Monday morning by specialist crews, there to dismantle the garages and hospitality units.

For me, I expect my Sunday to be somewhere around a fourteen-to-fifteen-hour day, before packing my case, grabbing a beer with my teammates, and flying to the next destination the following morning. Mere hours after the flag has dropped, the circus is on the road again: it's quite an incredible logistical feat. This has been my life for the last thirteen years!

CHAPTER 7

The Art of the Pitstop

All the way back in 2009, when I had the opportunity to walk down the pitlane prior to the Silverstone Grand Prix, my first ever time at a race, I set myself two rather ambitious goals. The first was that I wanted to travel the world, building Formula One cars for a living. The second, but for me probably the most important, was that I wanted to do pitstops. I remember watching various teams doing pitstop practice prior to that race in Silverstone. It was the moment at which my interest was well and truly sparked.

Formula One pitstops are always one of the very first things people ask me about when I discuss my job, and I can perfectly understand why. As a feat of both engineering and human performance, it's quite an insane undertaking when you think about it. A driver is going to drive down the pitlane at around 60 km/h. They're then going stop the car in a painted box on the ground that's almost exactly the same size as the car. That box is surrounded by eighteen people, who are then going to jack the car up into the air, change all four wheels, adjust the angle of the front wing flap and then drop the car back onto the ground, allowing the driver to drive out of the other side of the box. If everything goes to plan, all of this could be achieved in under two seconds. It is amazing.

Even today, when I think about pitstops like that, or break it down to all the individual stages of a modern F1 pitstop, I'm reminded that it's easy to become a little numb or unappreciative of what a feat it is to pull off the 'perfect' stop. I use inverted commas because, in my view, there really is no perfect stop. I recall when we broke the world record in Germany in 2019, turning Max Verstappen around in 1.88 seconds. Shortly after giving ourselves a thoroughly deserved pat on the back, everyone was analysing the footage and data, and almost immediately pointing out where we could have been sharper, more precise, essentially faster. That same mentality that the drivers have to get every bit of performance out of the car is mirrored by a great pit crew. The pitlane is our time to shine, and we revel in it. So, while we accept that it may be unlikely that a pitstop that's a half-second quicker or slower is going to have much impact on the race result, we're in the business of winning and that mentality has to apply throughout the entire operation in order to ensure its success. It's that

I was a bit of a handful as a kid – full of energy. That toy car would keep me occupied in the garden for hours.

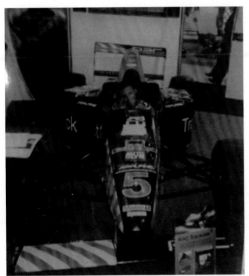

One of my first interactions with a race car. I can't remember the venue, but I was obviously enjoying myself.

My earliest motorsport photo, aged around eight, at a karting circuit near Reading. Health and Safety clearly wasn't a primary concern in those days, but I absolutely loved this place.

Taken at my first ever race working as a mechanic, the Britcar 24hr at Silverstone in 2010. The Honda Integra DC4 came back with plenty of battle scars, but it didn't miss a beat.

The lights of the Britcar pitlane in the middle of the night. There's something very special about night racing that always gives me a buzz.

Young and enthusiastic: this was during the early weeks of my time at The National College for Motorsport, when I was learning the basics of how to run a race car.

An early introduction to single-seaters at a college outing to Silverstone to run one of the Formula BMW cars.

Enduring the heat of a pre-season GP3 test in Spain.

The Lola B12/80 that Status GP entered into the 2012 European Le Mans Series. This was one of my favourite projects prior to taking on my first Formula One opportunity.

My first taste of Formula One: sitting in the MR02 at Goodwood during fire-up.

My final laugh with Jules. I feel very lucky that this photo exists so that I can remember all the smiles he brought to those around him.

Taken shortly after the chequered flag at the 2021 Abu Dhabi GP. It was the end of my toughest season in Formula One, and the range of emotions that we all went through that day will never be rivalled.

The day that Max Verstappen became Formula One's youngest race winner, in his debut with the team, Barcelona 2016.

Monaco 2015 with my partner, Phoebe. A time when we were both young, unencumbered and making the most of life on the road.

Waiting for the cars to arrive at the back of the grid. I've always used this time to find my focus and prepare for that first pitstop of the race. *(Mark Thompson/Getty Images)*

Celebrating Max Verstappen's win at the 2024 Brazilian Grand Prix. This win, after an incredible drive in wet weather conditions, would be championship defining and all but seal the 2024 Drivers' Championship for Max. *(Mark Thompson/Getty Images)*

attitude that led us to go on and break the world record yet again later in the season, finally setting a new world record for a Formula One pitstop of 1.82 seconds at the 2019 Brazilian Grand Prix.

With the regulations surrounding pitstops changing during the 2021 season and the 2022 regulations bringing larger, heavier wheels, the task of beating that world record became much tougher. With each accomplishment, your goals grow, though, so I'm sure that I'm not the only one who is a little annoyed that we haven't yet broken the 1.8-second mark. We knew that beating our record of 1.82 seconds was achievable, so to see McLaren pip us to it with a swift 1.8-seconds-dead pitstop at the 2023 Qatar Grand Prix was pretty painful. Even though we won the pitstop championship that year for a record sixth consecutive season, the loss of that world record left a bitter taste all around. It still does.

Being a part of the crew that owned that record for so long is most definitely one of my proudest achievements in racing. Mentioning that I was a world record holder was also my favourite annoying retort to my partner, Phoebe, whenever I was being berated for fucking something up, or just being generally incompetent or lazy at home. It's heartbreaking for me that I can no longer say this to her. In fact, I think it was one of the first things that came to my mind when I saw that our record had fallen.

I agree wholeheartedly with Michael Schumacher's view that 'records are made to be broken'. I guess the silver lining is that I believe that it is possible to complete a stop in 1.75 seconds: the team has achieved it in practice many times. The quickest stop that we've ever achieved in practice is closer to the 1.7 mark. As I look around my office at the plaques for pitstop championships over the years, it is more than a little frustrating that only nine of the ten fastest pitstops ever accomplished were performed by us. Is it a little ridiculous to focus on those imperfections? Perhaps, but over the years the whole thing has become a bit of an addiction.

When I set the goal for myself of wanting to be on a Formula One pit crew back in 2009, I simply wanted to participate as a crew member and to be good at it. Never at that point had I even considered that I could be a part of what is undoubtedly the best pit crew the sport has ever seen. At that point in my life, I hadn't fully rediscovered my competitive nature yet. It probably wasn't until 2015, upon meeting my new colleagues at Red Bull Racing and understanding what drove them, that this part of my own personality was truly reignited. With the support of this amazingly talented group of people, it became clear that there was the potential to keep finding time, with the goal being to achieve and ultimately break records.

So how does it all work? How is it made possible?

Well, like pretty much everything in Formula One, it's multi-faceted. It involves the engineering and design of the car and equipment; human performance, both physical and cognitive; and a host of external influences. These are just some of the factors that contribute to the success or failure of each pitstop. Some of these elements are within your control, but while carrying out your particular role at each pitstop, many are not. I guess with the latter, there are some elements of luck that will play a part.

Sporting director Jonathan Wheatley, who took responsibility for the crew and pitstops, often used the phrase 'control the controllables'. We used to quietly joke about these amusing little phrases that Jonathan would come out with each week but, being completely honest, his influence was undeniable and I don't think that in all my time racing I've ever met a fiercer competitor.

The design and engineering hours (and money, prior to the cost cap) that are invested into pitstops ensure that not only is the equipment specifically designed and modified to the users' needs, but the car also features elements specifically geared towards making pitstops faster, down to the smallest detail. The axles and wheel nuts, brake drums, locking mechanisms, the ergonomic shrouds on the wheel guns and positioning of the switches on the gun itself . . . all of these things have taken their design direction from the feedback given by the pit crew over many years.

Wheel-nut and axle design is, for me, one of the greatest strengths of the Red Bull cars with regard to pitstop performance. It is impossible, and I mean impossible, to cross-thread a Red Bull wheel nut or to 'round-off' the outside surfaces through operator error. This is the result of thousands of hours of research and development.

So, let's start with the axles and threads. It only takes three full turns of a nut for a wheel to be fully undone or tightened, as it is a very coarse thread. With the speed that a pitstop wheel gun achieves, and its ability to reach such high torque figures within just three hammer strikes, this coarse thread means that, as a wheel-gun operator, I never felt I had to be concerned that the nut wasn't tight enough. Even before the sensor-laden guns and data-logging equipment we use now came into play, the design itself instils confidence. So much so that once we did have all of those sensors and lights on the guns that denoted what stage of the pitstop you were in, the gun operators were still essentially working by feel. I'd feel the handle of the gun react in the opposite direction that the socket was spinning and I'd know the job was complete. I'd know, when I felt that torque reaction, that there was no chance that a nut was cross-threaded: it had to be seated correctly. It became a completely ingrained part of my muscle memory. Red Bull's 'dark' pitstop challenge, where the crew performed pitstops in complete darkness, is a great example of what I'm talking about. The video can be found on YouTube and I strongly recommend it as a demonstration of what great muscle memory looks like.

*

Next, there are the wheel nuts themselves, or more specifically the castellations on the outside of them. Wheel-nut design varies greatly up and down the pitlane but the titanium Red Bull nuts, in my view, are the best you'll ever see. The nuts only have five castellations, but the sockets have many internally. This means that the socket can engage on the nut in almost any position, avoiding what would be described as a 'dog-to-dog', where two of the castellations clash directly with one another, rather than interlocking as intended.

The design also allows the gun operator to chase the nut in as the car approaches. You can engage the socket on to a wheel nut very early, before the car has come to a complete stop, because even if the socket isn't quite square to the axle when you pull the trigger, you can usually get away with it. The socket is capable of engaging successfully at some pretty extreme angles. You might, however, on occasion, push this a little too far and end up with a Diwali-esque firework show in the pitlane. As the sparks would pepper your teammates and the noise would inevitably attract the attention of the cameramen in the pitlane, you'd know that the Sky Sports slow-motion shot of your failure was going to be everybody in the team's favourite Instagram reel for the next week. Thankfully, this really is quite rare.

During the years when lots of teams, including Red Bull, were running what were known as 'blown' front axles, it forced an unwelcome change to the wheel-nut design. The aerodynamic design intent of the axles necessitated that a much larger diameter wheel nut be used on the front of the car, with a much larger socket on the front wheel guns. This was a hurdle to be overcome in itself. For one, this larger socket made the gun a fair bit heavier and more awkwardly shaped. The large nuts themselves were also an issue. Because the 'blown' front axles needed to have a hollow section all the way through them, there was no space to put the wheel locking mechanisms. These are the small, spring-loaded tabs, or 'pawls', that are usually seen on the ends of the axle. Traditionally, as the gun socket would engage on the nut, these tabs were compressed into the axle by the socket, allowing the nut to slide over them. They exist to prevent a wheel from coming fully away from the axle should a nut come loose on-track. As they are a safety requirement, mandated by the FIA technical regulations, they too had to be moved away from the design of the axle and into the design of the new nut.

Any new design is likely to have its teething problems and this was no exception. It's quite unusual to have spring-loaded and moveable parts within a wheel-nut design and throughout pre-season testing and pitstop practice we had a myriad of issues related to the nuts. By the first race of the season, the design office had done a decent job of ironing most of these issues out, but for the pitstop gun operators, there was still a fundamental issue. We discovered that, on the wheel-off phase of the pitstop, with the spring-loaded locking mechanisms now being part of the nut assembly, rather than the axle, you ran a high risk of not releasing

THE ART OF THE PITSTOP

them for long enough for the nut to be freed from the axle thread if the gunman were to disengage the socket from the nut too early. Furthermore, if the nuts really failed, they would become impossible to remove entirely.

This was something that we learned the hard way on the Sunday morning of the 2015 Monaco GP. During our usual pre-race pitstop practice, a wheel nut decided that it didn't want to be undone, ever again. So, with around an hour to go until the pitlane opened for the cars to make their way to the grid, we found ourselves using an angle grinder to cut a wheel off one of the corners of an RB11, with all of the VIP guests in the pitlane watching on.

Even as late as 2021, a few teams, Mercedes included, were still running a 'key and hole'-philosophy wheel nut, whereby the flat area of the nut that was visible around the axle end featured multiple small recesses into which the 'teeth' on the gun socket slotted. It was quite an old design philosophy – I'd used similar nuts during my time at Marussia, back before wheel nuts were retained in the wheel. This is one of the areas to which I'd attribute the difference in performance between us and our competitors. The design of this type of nut was almost certainly the cause of the failure that led to the retirement of Valtteri Bottas's Mercedes from the Monaco GP in 2021. That incident's now often referred to as the 'forty-eight-hour pitstop', where even post-race, trackside technicians were unable to remove the wheel from Valtteri's car and, instead, shipped the stricken chassis back to Brackley, where the wheel was removed the following day.

The problem with this design is that if the wheel socket is not engaged perfectly square on to the nut, with all of the teeth fully inside all of the holes, you run the risk of stripping the material between the teeth out of the nut, thus rendering the nut impossible to remove. This is what happened to Valtteri on that day, with the mechanic trying to somehow get the socket to engage with enough material to unfasten the nut, but to no avail.

If you watched the Mercedes gun operators for the rest of that 2021 season, and all the way through 2022, you'll have noticed that they did not chase the axles in at all, as the Red Bull, Ferrari and McLaren crews did, trying to further shorten the time it took to complete the change. In a perfect pitstop, the nuts are already unfastened by the time the car has come to a complete stop and the jacks have been engaged. This means that as soon as the contact patch of the tyre leaves the ground as the car is lifted, the wheel can start to slide off the axle. We do this in an effort to find every hundredth of a second, ensuring that the car's stationary time is as short as possible. Before Mercedes made design changes to their wheel nuts and gun sockets for the 2023 season, you'll see that their gun operators waited until the car had completely stopped before engaging the sockets on to the nuts. They did this under instruction, as a way to limit the possibility of a repeat of the Monaco incident. While this was time-costly, as it was two- to three-tenths of a second slower to get the old wheel off, it was a necessary compromise. What point is there in doing a sub-two second pitstop if the following one results in the car being retired?

You may ask, 'Why didn't Mercedes just pursue a better design?' I think the short answer to that is by the time it had become a serious issue, everybody was operating under the new FIA financial regulations: the cost cap. Changing the nuts would have likely required some sort of change to the axles, and that would have required extensive testing and approval. I imagine that they simply decided that the amount of budget required to achieve it simply wasn't worth gaining half a second in the pitlane. They were probably right. During their years of domination from 2014 to 2020, pitstop performance was never likely to be a deciding factor in Mercedes's race results. With incredible reliability and outright speed, they didn't need to pour resources into pitstop performance. They were very reliable in the pitlane and that was all that was required. It wasn't until 2021, when the championship battle became ever increasingly tense, that it became a problem. As the Mercedes pit crew started to chase performance, to aid them in the championship battle, these small cracks started to show. While we were regularly completing stops in under two seconds, sometimes gaining a second on our competitors, they had no reply.

It was around this time that some of our competitors decided that rather than try to compete, it would be far easier to lobby the FIA to introduce regulations aimed at slowing us (and others) down. Under the guise of trying to improve pitlane safety, some teams argued to the governing body that Red Bull pitstops were essentially becoming dangerously fast, that it was only a matter of time until a car was released with a loose wheel.

The new rules regarding pitstops were largely focused around how the software that controls the release system is supposed to operate. Somewhere around 2017, when wheel guns first started using software that triggered the release of the jacks and control of the 'traffic light', there were rightfully concerns about how safe the process was and how automated these release systems can be. A Ferrari mechanic suffered a horrible, leg-breaking accident in the 2018 Bahrain Grand Prix as the result of the failure of an automated release system.

At the time, the wheel guns and software that the team were using didn't require the operator to independently confirm they were happy with the stop. At the beginning of the sequence, the nut was gunned off. The sensors in the gun recognised that the nut had been gunned off, and by operating a solenoid inside the gun, pushed the internal shuttle across, switching the gun to the 'tighten' phase. When the second nut was then gunned on, the sensors inside the gun counted the number of 'hammer' strikes and the number of turns the socket had made. When both of these criteria were met, the gun was then happy that the wheel nut was secure, with no other human input. When all four corners were complete, the car was released.

Where it had gone wrong for Ferrari was that the software couldn't account for anything other than a perfectly executed pitstop. In Bahrain, when the mechanic operating the rear-left gun tried to undo the wheel, it didn't come all the way off and the nut was still partially on the thread. In the past, before the wheel guns had this automatic direction-switching function, you would have simply re-engaged the socket and pulled the trigger again. However, in this instance, because the software in the gun believed that the first nut had come off, it had already switched directions. This meant that when the mechanic pulled the trigger for the second time, in an attempt to free the nut from the last thread, the gun instead nailed the old wheel back on to the axle. As a result of the software in the gun essentially 'believing' that the wheel change had been completed successfully, the moment the mechanic retightened that old wheel nut, the jacks were released and the light turned green. The mechanic had no method by which to stop the car from being released and Kimi Räikkönen, through no real fault of his own, pulled out of the pit box, running over the mechanic still standing in front of the rear-left tyre and breaking his leg.

This method, without an ultimate human-controlled override for the release, was almost immediately banned by the FIA after the Bahrain accident. At Red Bull Racing, the guns we were using around this time did have a manually operated 'confirm' button, but we used it like a dead man's switch. As long as the button was held throughout the stop, the car would release from the pit box once complete. We would only release this button if and when something went awry during the course of a wheel change, pressing it again once we were satisfied that all was well. It was a much safer system and we'd proven it out. However, this method was something that the new FIA regulations outlawed. The confirm button can no longer be pressed and held throughout the process; rather, it can only be pressed after the light on the wheel gun goes green to confirm that the nut is tight. If you press the button too early, the green light will flash and you'll have to release the button and reconfirm before the car will be released.

Along with this new set of regulations was also the requirement for teams to introduce delays between the confirmation of the wheel changes and the release of the jacks, and the traffic light going green.

I don't think I've spoken to anyone in the pitlane or anyone watching races at home who believes these latest regulations have made pitlane safety any better or improved the spectacle of pitstops for fans. With regard to safety, there are plenty of arguments against the new rules. The first is that, in an attempt to dissuade the FIA from making these punitive rule changes, Red Bull proved through various experiments that even if the torque or depth sensors in the gun did fail, they would always fail safe. This meant that in all circumstances, even with a gun or software failure of any sort, the car couldn't leave with a loose wheel. The result would be that the car would not drop from the jacks and the traffic light would stay red.

A second point is that the FIA change in relation to the confirm button only resulted in giving the crew about an extra tenth or two of a second to stop the process. If a pit-crew member does think that something has gone awry, there's absolutely no chance that an additional tenth of a second is going to be sufficient to react to that and prevent the car from driving away. As I said earlier, the fastest gunmen aren't looking at the lights on their gun before pressing the confirm button anyway, they're operating on feel alone. I used to look at the light as an afterthought, so there's no way that the extra tenth would be long enough for me to see a problem and react quickly enough to remove my finger from the confirm button. In order for this kind of delay to be effective, and prevent a car from being released in an unsafe condition, it would have to be closer to a second, or we'd need to introduce a minimum stop time, neither of which would be welcome.

Joyfully for my argument (but less so for the Williams pit crew), the footage of the unsafe release of Alexander Albon's car at the 2024 Imola GP shows just how useless these software delays are in preventing a car from being released with a loose wheel. In that pitstop, I can only assume a software failure allowed the car to drop initially. But you can see from the footage that despite the couple of tenths of a second in delay, once the mechanic on the front-right had recognised the problem, he had absolutely no chance of preventing the car from being released from the pit box.

The other issue with these rule changes and the delays introduced is, in my view, that it has made the job of the pitlane spotter, the person ultimately responsible for making sure a car isn't released into the path of another, far more difficult. Imagine trying to watch a pitstop, checking that all four corners are progressing as expected while also keeping one eye down the pitlane for any approaching traffic – not an easy job. Now imagine also having to factor into your release a delay between completion of the four corners and the car dropping off the jacks and then a further delay between that and the light going green. It would be interesting to see how many more incidents of close calls between cars entering and leaving pits we have had since the introduction of these delays. It seems to happen almost every week now.

As much as it has irked me, and robbed fans of witnessing super-fast stops, I understand why the FIA felt they had to take action. When people use 'safety' concerns as a political tool or for sporting advantage, it puts the governing body in a tight spot. If they take no action, it puts them in the firing line if something were to go wrong anytime from then onwards. The truth is, though, the last time Red Bull left the pit box with a loose wheel was way back in 2013, when the average pitstop time was way higher than we see now. The faster pace of the pitstops hadn't contributed to any more failures. So, if the delays do nothing to improve safety, and nothing for the spectacle for fans, you have to ask why they were really introduced in the first place.

The wheel guns at Red Bull Racing are quite the work of art. Red Bull, similarly to all the other teams, buy an off-the-shelf pneumatic wheel gun from Paoli, the leading manufacturer in the field. We then take it entirely apart and modify the internal parts to suit our needs. We reduce its weight and make it spin faster and produce greater torque more quickly. It's then fitted with a multitude of torque, angle and depth sensors, pneumatically operated directional switches and lights for the operator to see what mode and what stage of the pitstop the gun was in. The whole thing is then covered in an ergonomic carbon shroud, which was created based on the feedback taken from gun operators over the many years that Red Bull has been pursuing excellence in that field. Every couple of years, Paoli come along with a new gun design with better initial performance and the process repeats itself.

Lots of people on social media have asked me over the years how the guns are operated and what all the lights and buttons do, so it would be rude of me not to enlighten you. The operation of the guns isn't overly complicated. I understand that it's easy to say this after a decade of doing it, but in terms of the actual function for the user, the design had a mandate of being simple and intuitive. There are three main functional switches on the gun that you need to operate.

The first of those is the trigger. Its function is fairly simple: it opens the internal port allowing high pressure air (around 30 bar) to pass into the gun, making the socket spin. If you ever get the opportunity to hold a live F1 pitstop wheel gun, I recommend being fully prepared for both the noise and the torque reaction if you're going to pull the trigger. I'm pretty sure that if you did pull the trigger accidently, or were holding the gun in just one hand unprepared, you'd quickly find yourself on the way to the medical centre. I say this having myself spent an evening in a Barcelona hospital during my first year at Marussia, while my thumb was stitched back together. Wheel guns are serious bits of kit; they're heavy, powerful and loud. In all my time at Red Bull, I'm pretty sure the only guest we ever encouraged to pull the trigger was the actor and former American football star Terry Crews, and he swiftly declined. It was a wise decision; his nice white shirt would've been completely ruined by the oil in the air lines.

The second switch is the directional toggle, positioned just forward of the trigger. This switch isn't actually used during the course of a pitstop. Rather, it's used to reset the gun to the 'undo' phase at the end of a stop, or the user can pull the switch the other way and the gun will change to 'tighten'. During a stop, some electronic and pneumatic wizardry uses the sensors to determine that you have undone the nut and the gun then switches direction automatically. This allows the user simply to engage the socket on to the second nut and pull the trigger again to tighten it.

It was a huge development that only arrived in the later years of my time on the crew. When we first started testing it and ironed out the bugs, we knew that it was a game changer. When I did my first live pitstop as a member of the Marussia crew back in 2013, you still had to bang the shuttle on your leg to switch the direction of the gun during the stop. That's how it had been for many years. I remember waking up the morning after my first ever pitstop practice back at Status GP and it taking me a while to work out why my leg was sore; it wasn't until I saw that my right thigh was one giant bruise from repeatedly smashing a piece of metal into my leg that I realised what an impact the job was going to have on me physically. When I first arrived at Red Bull, the directional shuttle was pneumatically powered but you had to physically flick the switch mid-stop to make it switch over.

When the auto switch was introduced, it meant that you could keep your focus entirely on the axle and nut without any distraction or without changing your hand position to flick a switch. These small gains were everything when we were chasing a sub-two-second stop.

The final thing you need to operate on the gun is the confirm button: a simple press and hold with your left thumb once the wheel change was complete. As explained, prior to the 2021 pitstop rule changes, we could treat this button like a dead man's switch, holding it down throughout the pitstop and only releasing it in the event that something was going wrong, which would prevent the car from dropping and being released.

There is also a series of LEDs built in to the shroud of the gun, each one denoting a different stage of the pitstop and the status of the wheel gun. First yellow, which denotes which mode the gun is in: solid yellow for 'undo' and flashing for 'tighten'. Then there is red, which only appears if the gun's sensors determine that the nut is not tight enough at the end of the stop. It usually means that the gun operator simply hasn't allowed enough trigger time for the hammer action of the gun to tighten the nut enough.

Getting a red light at the end of a pitstop is one of the worst things that can happen from the gun operator's perspective. It means that you have to re-engage on the nut, pull the trigger again to tighten the nut further, and then reconfirm with your thumb. If this happens, it usually costs you just over a second, which might not sound like a lot of time, but if your average time for the entire pitstop is less than two and a half seconds, that loss as a percentage becomes a lot more significant. In the worst-case scenario, a red light can also indicate a wheel gun failure, which would require reaching for the spare gun to complete the pitstop, probably costing four or five seconds. This is an absolute nightmare.

Finally, a solid green light tells the operator that the stop is complete, the nut is tight, and this is confirmed with the push button. If, however, the green light flashes, it means that the gun is happy that the nut is tight and that physically everything is fine, but that the operator has pressed the confirm button too early. This feature is the later addition that was born out of the regulations introduced by the FIA, at the behest of our competitors, to slow down our pitstops.

We adapted to the change fairly quickly and, as explained, the data has revealed that this reaction and manual confirmation costs each corner only between one- and two-tenths of a second. We discovered fairly quickly that it simply wasn't worth pushing our luck with the confirm button. Yes, you may be able to gain a few hundredths of a second by being faster to push it but, if you go early, it costs around three- to five-tenths while you react to the flashing light, release the button and reconfirm.

The development of pitstop equipment, much like in the performance areas of the cars, has constantly progressed during my time at Red Bull, but it was curtailed drastically when the cost cap came into force. I remember Jonathan Wheatley telling us to get any changes we needed recorded and into the design phase the year before the cap came into play, because they weren't going to happen afterwards. You can perfectly understand why teams had to make these compromises due to the cost cap. Gaining a tenth in a pitstop could never be a priority for a team over outright car performance, but it was a shame nonetheless.

From the perspective of us in the pitlane, we're competing for pride. We certainly aren't doing it for the money. I've seen some outlandish figures thrown around over the years in regard to how much pit-crew personnel earn. The truth is, we don't earn any more for being on the pit crew. It's something that you do in addition to your role as a mechanic or technician. I always felt that this was a little unfair considering it meant far more strenuous work in some tough conditions, extra time for practices, functional fitness and dealing with pressures that others simply do not have. Not only that, but in the six consecutive years that Red Bull Racing won the DHL Pitstop Challenge, we've never received a bonus for it. There's actually no financial incentive to be on the crew at all: people do it because they love it. For comparison, in Indy Car, the winning pitstop challenge crew are awarded around $50,000 to be split between them.

There was a long-running joke among the pit crew that the team did in fact get a cash prize for winning the pitstop challenge each year, but Jonathan Wheatley kept it to himself. It did seem suspicious that each year we won, he seemed to buy himself another new Porsche. I regularly joked about this with him. On one occasion, I said to him that if he was going to keep all the prize money, perhaps his new GT3RS should become a timeshare and that each member of the team could schedule a week-long holiday in it over the year.

The design intent of both the car and the pitstop equipment is part of the picture when discussing Red Bull Racing's dominance in the pitlane for the last seven years. The other part, in my view the larger influence on the team's success in this area, is human performance. When I first started at Red Bull, I would have said that all of the more advanced equipment, compared to what I was accustomed to at Marussia, was the big differentiator between the performance of pit crews up and down the paddock. Back in 2015, that may have been the case to some extent, but it doesn't paint a complete picture. By the time we got to 2018, most teams were using equivalent or, in the case of some other big teams, better equipment. The Mercedes wheel guns seem to run at higher pressure and spin faster than ours. The Ferrari wheel nuts seemed to tighten almost instantly and their rear jack is very simple and quick to get the car in the air. Despite this, we retained the honour of calling ourselves the fastest pit crew and winning the DHL Pitstop Challenge six years running.

In my view, that is because, for us, simple human performance was the primary influence on our pitstop times. Skill, drive, mental fortitude: these are the areas where we beat our competition. Jonathan Wheatley often used to refer to it as a 'ground war' and, while we all used to find it quite amusing, essentially, he was right. Consistently delivering the fastest pitstops over the course of six consecutive seasons isn't something that can be attributed to the equipment or design features of the

LIFE IN THE PITLANE

car alone. Even throughout various changes of rules and regulations, changes in crew personnel and the constant pressure of competing at the sharp end of the grid, Red Bull Racing have been the benchmark for performance in the pitlane for as long as I can remember.

Bear in mind that pitstops, as part of the bigger picture of trying to win world championships, are a pretty low priority for many seniors in the team. Paul Monaghan used to regularly mock Jonathan's obsession with pitstop performance. From a race strategy point of view, there really was little benefit in chasing 1.8-second pitstops and increasing the risk of the kind of disaster that we witnessed outside the Mercedes garage in Monaco during the 2021 season. He and most of the engineering and strategy team would be perfectly happy with a season full of uneventful 2.5-second pitstops.

The thing is, though, there aren't many instances where those of us working behind the scenes get the opportunity to be recognised by the public for our skill and dedication, and the pitlane is our time to shine; that's the reason it is so important to us. Also, while the gains in each round of pitstops might be fairly minimal, perhaps two-tenths to half a second, over the course of a three-stop race, it adds up. In the years of chasing every point possible, in a battle for second place behind the dominant Mercedes, these small gains often helped us in terms of valuable track position over our rivals.

What's more important than outright speed of any one pitstop is consistency. There's really no point in being able

174

to do a sub two-second pitstop if the next two are disastrous because people are trying too hard and the car ends up sitting in the box for five or six seconds. Consistency is key, and having a reliable pit crew helps the strategy group to plan accordingly. Knowing that, statistically, each pitstop will likely be somewhere between 1.8 and 2.2 seconds is useful knowledge when a strategist is trying to plan an undercut on a rival.

We've talked a lot at Red Bull Racing over the years about 'functional fitness' in order to maintain the high standards that we've set for ourselves. I guess what that actually means is open to interpretation (I've certainly interpreted it in my own way). It's easy to just picture a group of people in the gym every day, lifting weights and on treadmills, and while a fair bit of that does go on, it's never been something I'm particularly into. I just cannot get on with the gym. I've tried and I just find that it brings me absolutely zero pleasure – not over any period of time anyway. I've flirted with it in the past but I just find the whole thing so incredibly boring.

The only time that I've ever spent any prolonged period in the gym was in my first year at Red Bull as a member of the support team. The support team, as it was called at the time, was the crew of mechanics that travelled to the various Red Bull show events throughout the course of the year. Usually running the RB7 or RB8, it was a pretty cool gig. It was low pressure, fun and you got to go to some cool places. The Kitzbühel mountain run in Austria with Max Verstappen, the zero-gravity pitstop and an incredible Bollywood film set in Hyderabad, India, were just some of the places I was able to visit prior to joining the race team.

The idea of the support team was that you could get used to the operational procedures at the team in a low-pressure environment while preparing for a role on the race team when the opportunity arose. The other nice thing about the support team was that you assisted the race team by helping with the car build whenever they were back in the factory in Milton Keynes, as well as doing night shifts during pre-season testing, along with any in-season tyre testing or filming days.

The year I spent on the support team was unusually quiet, with large gaps between events. I used the downtime to get in the gym, sometimes twice a day. One of the privileges of being in a travelling role with Red Bull Racing is that nobody will have an issue with you spending time in the gym during work hours; in fact, it is encouraged, all in the name of pitstop performance. Unless you're an athlete, there aren't many jobs out there where you'll get paid to go and spend time in the gym improving your physical fitness.

When I joined the team in January 2015, I was admittedly a little overweight, the heaviest I'd ever been, clocking in at a hefty 103 kg. By the time I joined the race team in 2016, I was 84 kg and in my best physical shape since I was sixteen and playing sport daily. The Marussia years hadn't been particularly kind to me. There really was no big expectation to keep fit and the drinking culture had taken its toll. I spent my first six months at Red Bull trying to shake it off, and I did. However, once I got back to the racetrack, the long days soon took all of my spare energy and my interest in the gym waned fairly quickly.

I'm still in awe of my colleagues that can do a fourteen-hour day and then somehow find the willpower and energy to do a full workout. Thankfully, as a gun operator, I always felt that physical shape wasn't really a huge issue for the role I was performing. I'm fortunate enough to have a genetic predisposition to the role, with large arms and shoulders, and although I pile on a bit of extra timber if I don't stay active, I tend to maintain muscle mass well enough without spending hours in the gym. I guess I should thank my dad for passing on this trait.

Wheel off/wheel on and the front and rear jacks are by far the most physically demanding jobs on a Formula One pit crew, particularly since the new, larger wheels were introduced in 2022. It's back-breaking work just running them in and out of the garage. When I started on the rear right wheel gun, I discovered very quickly that the physical requirements were going to be far easier to cope with than the mental ones. Even after years of experience, I will still say that, rather than my physical condition, it is my mental state on any given Sunday that will likely determine my pitstop performance, even down to my mood. Because of this, I've tended, over the years, to concentrate any training

I did do on things like my reactions, focus and dealing with pressure while remaining calm.

There are so many things to combat when you step into a pitlane during a race with fifteen seconds' notice before the car arrives and you have to perform your role: nerves, anxiety, pressures both internal and external, the noise, the distractions. All of these things can impact your performance, potentially catastrophically if you haven't got them under control. You have to have a handle on them, and all while experiencing a huge rush of adrenaline. After a decade of experience, I don't like to pretend that these issues don't affect me. Rather, I feel like I use them for good rather than allowing them to hamper my performance.

There are many ways in which the team trainers try to help us condition our minds in order to overcome the pressures we face in the pitlane. Some of these I have found helpful, but the trainers also understand that we are all very different people with different mindsets and, as such, things that work for some simply wouldn't for others.

One of the techniques that trainers seemed quite keen on was absolutely never going to work for me. Starting around 2020, we were asked to try and use 'visualisation' as a way of preparing our minds for pitstops. We'd start by sitting, closing our eyes and taking a few deep breaths, supposedly clearing our minds before visualising the series of events leading up to the pitstop, followed by the pitstop itself. This was a total waste of time for me and I was quite outspoken about my feeling that the whole thing was complete bullshit. For starters, as a crew we'd been on an incredible run of form in the pitlane already: in 2018–19 there wasn't a crew that could even claim to be close to what we were doing each week. We'd broken our own world record three times in almost as many races and destroyed the competition in the pitlane the season before. Rather than sweating it out in the gym trying to build muscle, or 'visualising' doing the job, I'd always prefer to work on my reactions and accuracy.

I found that one way I could get the best out of myself was to play to what I knew about my own personality already, in particular, my love of competition. While it's absolutely true that it takes the entire crew to perform simultaneously in order for a pitstop to be successful, it is also true that the only thing I can have any impact on in the pitlane is my own performance. As such, one of the things that I used to do was consider my corner on the rear-right almost as if it was its own team and that we were in competition with the other three corners of the car. At the end of the day, a pitstop can only be as fast as the slowest corner to be completed. So, the first target was to never be the slowest corner.

Thankfully, in the world of wheel guns that are full of sensors and provide data related to each stage of a pitstop, I had a perfect tool with which to gauge my corner's performance against the other three. Gun operators at Red Bull also all wear helmet cameras during the race, for the purpose of analysis and fault-finding should something go wrong. Some of the footage is absolutely incredible. When you see the precision with which the socket meets the nut in a perfect stop and the timing of the wheel off/wheel on sequence in perfect synchronicity with the engagement of the jacks, it almost looks robotic. As well as having those video recordings of each and every pitstop we did, in both practice and the race, we also had in the factory what I referred to as 'the screen of truth', a monitor that at the end of each stop would show the completion time for each corner.

As I'm sure you can imagine, when this screen was introduced, the competition among the corner crews began almost immediately, as did a lot of banter. Each week, the WhatsApp group with me and the three other gun operators would be filled with braggadocio from whoever had put in the best performance at the previous race, plus excuses from whoever had been the slowest according to the data. One of the only reasons I would open my laptop between races would be to see if the report from the previous week's pitstops had been completed and, on a particularly good week, I'd be straight on the phone to give the other guys some grief. My counterparts on the other corners would do exactly the same if they'd had a good week. I loved it!

Despite being well beyond 10,000 hours of practical experience, it's probably only in the last couple of years where I can say that I've mastered all of the stresses of that first pitstop on a Sunday. Up until just a few years ago there were still days where I might allow an intrusive thought, an unfortunate event or experience prior to the race, or even just getting up on the wrong side of the bed to have at least a small impact on my day in the pitlane. At this point, I can confidently say that I can step out in any pitlane under any circumstance and perform under pressure. It has taken a long time and a lot of learning.

One of the hardest things to do is to refocus after things have gone wrong. The margins are so fine when you're trying to operate at that level that there will inevitably be failures. When it happens, the best people can recover quickly. I always used to say that if my 'bad' stops were under 3.5 seconds, that's a perfectly good recovery. It takes a great deal of adaptability to recover from a mistake in such a short period.

I've made plenty of mistakes in the pitlane. When I made one soon after I'd taken on the wheel-gun role, it went really badly, leaving Sergio Pérez sitting in the pit box for around ten seconds as I scrambled to rectify the issue. On my best day, I was probably just as fast back then as I am now. The difference is that, now, my bad stops go largely unnoticed by the viewing public. When you see a Red Bull pitstop take three seconds, someone's had an issue, even if the TV commentators haven't seen it – those are the margins we're dealing with. That consistency only comes with experience; there is no replacement for it and it's vital when things do go wrong. That is why Jonathan Wheatley was always so protective of the crew and vehemently opposed to losing personnel from 'his' race team.

One of the things that I will always credit for my success in the pitlane is the team of people around me. In my eyes, every single member of that pit crew is undoubtably the very best at what they do. It's knowing that to be true and having the support of those around me that allowed me to perform at my best over such a long period of time.

Now, when the sporting director comes on the radio to announce, 'Pitstop imminent,' my mind is able to instantly forget anything else that is going on, ignore any other information and focus solely on the task at hand until the car drives away and the job is done. I know that if I do my job well, my teammates will do the same. For that brief period, while the car is right there in front of you, nothing else matters. It's amazing how hard it is and how long it takes to teach your brain to work like that. Tuning your senses to only focus on the information that matters is a very tough skill to master.

When I talk about the importance of focus, I often say to people that once I'm in the pitlane on my knees and watching the car come towards the box, pretty much anything could be going on around me and it wouldn't impact my performance. There could be a gang of pink elephants robbing the engineers on the pit wall of their phones and wallets at gunpoint and I probably wouldn't notice, so narrow is my field of vision. From the point that the car is 20 metres away, my eyes are fixated on the centre of that rear right wheel, and as the axle end becomes visible when the wheel moves in front of me, my arms extend almost automatically to engage the socket onto the nut.

I have a little mantra that plays over and over in my head as the car approaches: 'See the nut, hit the nut' – a little rhythmic phrase that I repeat over and over in my head as the car is approaching. This is the trigger to begin the perfectly choreographed dance that I and the two other mechanics on my corner will undertake as the race car rolls into the box.

After this many years in the job and the seemingly endless hours of practice, the physical skill has become almost autonomous; as I said earlier, it's muscle memory. I don't have to think about the action at all; rather, my conscious thoughts are centred on 'controlling the controllables'. Car positioning, wheel-gun failures or software issues, delays with any of the other corners . . . none of these things are within my control so there's absolutely no point in losing focus on the job thinking about them.

Over the years I've done various jobs on the pit crew both in F1 and WEC: wheel off/wheel on, fuelling, and driver swap. In some cases, I needed to go to the dreaded gym as there was a physical requirement in order for me to further improve performance. The biggest necessity is to avoid injury over the course of some very long seasons, which requires a certain level of physical fitness. I'd estimate that over the course of a season we'll do somewhere around a hundred live race pitstops. Then there's all the practice sessions, both in Milton Keynes and each day at the circuit. So, it's not hard to imagine the physical toll it takes on the body.

I make no qualms about it: it's a young person's game! At the ripe old age of thirty-five, you'll see that on any given weekend at least one of my limbs will have been strapped up by the long-serving team physio, John Hammond. Usually, it's a knee or an elbow. By the end of the year, it's often both. These things are part and parcel of the job but, as you get older, it certainly gets harder to shake off these little knocks.

Despite all the little injuries, the extra hours of practice and the stress, I still love it. I doubt that I'll ever experience anything that will compare to the pressure of being in the pitlane as a Formula One car approaches the box for its first stop in a close race. Equally, nothing beats the adrenaline rush and the sense of accomplishment when you absolutely nail it. Much like any other drug, that adrenaline is addictive and, when I do leave the pitlane for good, I'll have to find a healthy outlet to replace it.

CHAPTER 8

All Eyes on Us

When Bernie Ecclestone sold the management of Formula One to Liberty Media in January 2017, I don't think many in the paddock could see the extent to which, and just how quickly, the sport's reach and popularity would grow. In fact, it's only now, when I look back to my early years in the paddock before that sale, that I realise just how different the place was.

There weren't anywhere near the number of photographers and media outlets filling every corner of the paddock – the mob of photographers and content creators for teams' social media platforms didn't really exist. When you look back at the access to the sport at that time, and compare it to what we have now, it's almost as though the previous management were trying to keep the whole thing a secret. It shouldn't be a surprise at all that the sport was nowhere near as popular as it is today. Bernie had done a very good job of maintaining the image of an exclusive and elitist club. The paddock was far out of reach to the average sports fan. Instead, a Grand Prix was a great occasion to drink champagne with potential investors, preferably while ogling grid girls from a Monaco harbour yacht. Prior to Liberty Media, the sport, and certainly the F1 paddock, was the perfect definition of an 'old boys' club'. Media passes were closely guarded and only available to the few, and guest passes were all used by team sponsors or gifted to an elite club of old men who'd been in and around the paddock for ever.

When I first started travelling, teams were not constantly reaching out to fans and content creators in the way they do now, giving them the chance to see what they love up close, with brand exposure through social media understood as currency. In terms of its workforce, the paddock was made up almost entirely of one demographic: middle-aged, white European men. The Formula One job market of old also reeked of nepotism, and there were very few ways for those not already 'inside' the sport to have any opportunity to learn more about it, let alone become a part of it.

All of these things combined had made it hard for the sport to grow. For anyone unfamiliar with motorsport, it wasn't exactly inviting. Complicated rules and regulations, huge sums of money spent on technologies that often went largely unexplained, nobody with both access and permission to explain them, and very few opportunities for the public to get any real insight into the inner workings of the sport, its politics and the people behind the scenes.

Certainly, when I first started working in the paddock, a fairly common reaction when I told someone what I did for a living was, 'Oh, that's nice. I don't really know anything about it, to be honest.' I can't remember the last time I spoke to someone who had that reaction. Since 2017, the sport has exploded, with the 2021 season finale one of the most watched sporting events in the world.

The growth in popularity of Formula One has to be largely attributed to the strategies put in place by Liberty Media – the timing isn't just coincidence. I couldn't imagine the sport being where it is now under Bernie's reign, with him being so unwilling to embrace change. One of the first noticeable changes to the atmosphere surrounding the sport was what we could see immediately in front of us at the circuit. We noticed that race weekends slowly became more like festivals. With each season, circuits were hosting more and more entertainment outside the on-track activity: live music, hands-on experiences for spectators and a much wider effort to entertain more people for longer over the course of a three-day event. All of this was great and it made a noticeable change to the type of people we would see attending races throughout the year. One of the biggest parts of these strategies for growth was what we now refer to as 'the Netflix effect'.

When we were told at the start of the 2018 season that Netflix would be filming in the paddock for a new Formula One documentary, and that camera crews would be allowed into teams' garages to capture footage, the reaction was one of equal shock and excitement. In an industry that was understandably so protective over intellectual property, it seemed impossible that all of the teams would agree to this.

With that said, I wasn't surprised that Red Bull were all-in on the idea, or that Mercedes did not participate in the first season. With Red Bull being a business that now essentially sold a lifestyle heavily weighted on pushing the limits and doing the extreme, *Drive to Survive* was a perfect fit. Red Bull had clearly set its sights on conquering North America, and Netflix was going to be a great way to help them do that. Show runs in Mexico City, prior to a Formula One Grand Prix returning to the country in 2015 for the first time in twenty-three years, had already shown the enthusiasm for racing there, and with Austin fast becoming the most popular of the new races in an ever-expanding calendar, the stage was set for a North American explosion.

It was quite odd at first, having strange faces wielding cameras in the garage and seeing boom microphones suddenly appear above you when conversing with colleagues. It certainly made us all a little nervous to begin with. None of us wanted to give the production crew an out-of-context soundbite that could be used in the series and end up getting us in trouble. We guessed that the team would surely have the final sign-off of any content that was to be used, but we were still conscious that anything we did or said could end up being viewed by millions. It wasn't as though people were usually saying or doing anything particularly egregious in the garage over the course of the weekend, but as we were constantly getting up to mischief and making jokes that were usually private, it definitely took a little while for everyone to have enough trust in the production team that we could all relax and continue on as normal.

Certainly, the extra eyes and ears in the garage didn't go unnoticed. I remember early on, sitting outside hospitality in Australia with a few of the boys, having a laugh over breakfast, when a microphone suddenly appeared overhead. The laughter stopped and the table went completely silent for a moment before I broke it by loudly and deliberately commenting, 'God, all those Red Bull mechanics really deserve a pay rise and more holiday'. I turned to the microphone operator to see him laughing. He understood that the intrusion into our morning coffee wasn't particularly welcome and he duly left us alone.

As with any new addition to the garage, the various production crews were welcomed, though, and after a period, it just became the norm. Initially, the biggest imposition was simply having extra bodies in the limited workspace. Some of the garages that we operate out of over the year are pretty small already, so having extra people with camera equipment there was a little inconvenient. But soon enough, as those new faces learned how we operated and where not to stand, they weren't in the way any more. Today, we have more marketing, content, hospitality and communications personnel in the garage than ever before, and we've become completely used to the busy corridors and cameras and microphones in our workspace throughout the week.

I must admit, I was a fairly late adopter of social media. I didn't join Instagram until 2018 and although I had a Twitter account from 2012, it pretty much sat dormant until 2021. It wasn't until I found that my Instagram account was experiencing an odd and unexplainable growth in followers at some point during 2020 that I began to understand what a useful and powerful tool social media could be for me.

With the first season of *Drive to Survive* being shown in 2019 and growing in popularity as the years went on, I started regularly receiving messages from people on social media who had recognised me from the series and wanted to get in touch. Often the messages were from fans of the show who just wanted to tell me that they loved my on-screen reactions and that it was nice to see people who were so passionate about racing. It wasn't lost on me that I seemed to be so much more noticeable than the other technicians during *Drive to Survive*'s edited scenes. Why did I, a lowly technician, seem to get so much more screen time than others, even though my role in the team didn't warrant me becoming a main character in the series, and I certainly wasn't an influential figure in the sport or the paddock?

Not too long ago, I went back and rewatched some of the earlier series of *Drive to Survive*, and actually, in those first two seasons, I wouldn't say that I got much more screen time than others. When I look back and pick out my teammates' faces, they're all there; it was just that I stood out more than the others for one very obvious reason. It was very simple and, among us in the garage, it was something that we all knew and had discussed plenty of times before. As has been the case with so much of my time in racing, I was the only Black guy. I think this is probably why so many people sought to contact me on social media, something that at this point I had not fully embraced yet.

When *Drive to Survive* began filming, the paddock wasn't a particularly diverse place. Actually, that's probably being a bit too kind. It's more accurate to say that the paddock at that time wasn't in any measurable way diverse. It certainly wasn't in terms of the ethnicity or gender of those working in it, me and just a couple of others being the exception. I'm happy to say that it is an area where the sport is changing, albeit slowly. I remember talking to a colleague about the fact that the camera was always on me and, at the time, I wasn't particularly pleased about it. Had I been willing to ignore my view as to why I was always featured, it would have been easier to deal with, but my usually cynical brain was a little upset by the idea that my image was essentially being used to promote the sport as something that it wasn't: diverse and inclusive. On top of this, I felt that all of my colleagues deserved just as much recognition for their work, and I found it almost embarrassing that I'd become 'the Black mechanic with the dreads'.

It didn't help that it seemed to me that the team now suddenly wanted me to participate in every bit of content filming going. I imagined that someone in the marketing department had seen reactions on social media and the comments on certain posts asking who 'the Black guy' was, and there had been some sort of off-the-books meeting about how to leverage this. A secret meeting where someone had mentioned that it would be a great PR move to use my image to subconsciously promote the team as somehow being more diverse than others purely because I was trackside.

The thing that bugged me most about this imaginary scenario was that the team as a whole was way more diverse than any team I'd worked at previously, so I didn't understand why it would need to be advertised. I guess that *Drive to Survive* was seen as an opportunity to show people what life was like at the circuit, but it didn't give any insight into those who worked at the teams' UK bases. Race teams are such a small snapshot of those working in F1: just sixty trackside staff of the thousands employed by each team, but as I was some sort of rarity among the race team, Red Bull probably wanted to make the most of the opportunity.

*

One week, at breakfast in Azerbaijan, I was told by somebody on the marketing team that, for some team social media content, I'd be mic'd up for the week and that a film crew would be following me around to capture me in my role. As usual, I was sceptical, mostly because it's a bit of a pain in the arse whenever marketing ask you to do these features and spend a large portion of your day with a microphone tucked into your shirt. It's exhausting trying to remind yourself repeatedly throughout the day that your conversations are not private, that everything you say is being recorded. It's not that I feared saying anything particularly heinous, or that I wouldn't say in normal conversation, but I didn't have any media training, and it was possible that someone would hear a comment out of context and interpret it as something sinister or offensive. With social media becoming ever more powerful, I was beginning to become warier of how I presented myself, and being mic'd up all day made me feel quite vulnerable.

To make matters worse, I knew that once the rest of the garage was aware of this filming taking place, they were going to find great amusement in making my day more difficult. Having colleagues make lewd or generally embarrassing statements for the benefit of the microphone was par for the course whenever one of us was asked to create this kind of content for social media. I had fully enjoyed these shenanigans myself when they'd filmed a similar piece with a colleague a few weeks earlier. Having waited until I knew the mics were recording, I'd walked over to one of the No. 1 mechanics and asked him if he'd 'been given that haemorrhoid cream by the doctor'. Watching him go bright red and seeing the sound guy across the garage absolutely pissing himself was brilliant. I guess it was karma that it would end up being my turn next, and my teammates spent plenty of energy returning the favour.

If you watch that video on YouTube there is a little scene where I'm having what looks like a fairly technical conversation with then No. 1 mechanic Lee Stevenson. Actually, Lee had walked over and asked if I buttered my toast on both sides or just the one side. It was an odd interaction but, watching the video, you'd never know we were talking absolute nonsense.

This initial bit of personal exposure, in what became a short piece entitled *60 Seconds with Calum Nicholas* on Red Bull's channels, would be the first time I truly realised that social media could be a powerful tool when used to promote careers in racing. Reading the comments on YouTube, I saw just how important representation can be to help nurture a more diverse paddock, and while I still wasn't keen on diving head first into social media, the prospect of doing other things involved with the sport was exciting. The comment section on the *60 Seconds* video was full of young people expressing how refreshing it was to learn more about the people behind the scenes, and as the content spread across platforms I was inundated with messages from fans. Among these fans were large numbers of young Black and ethnic minority men and women telling me that they too love racing and engineering. Many explained that seeing me achieving my goals with a top team inspired them to pursue a career that they had previously viewed as out of reach. It was quite overwhelming.

Until then, I hadn't seen the benefit of trying to grow a platform and certainly didn't understand it all. However, an internal conflict began when I started reading people's kind messages. All these people had taken the time out of their day to find me and tell me that they appreciated seeing me on a screen, and I felt obliged to reply, even if just to say thank you . . . so, I did. Soon, people started asking questions about the path that I had taken to get to F1 and how I'd started out, and so I answered those questions too. A couple of years later, without realising, much like a frog in slowly boiling water, I had now apparently become a social media personality and, even scarier, a role model.

Even throughout most of 2020, I still barely posted on Instagram but the following just kept growing. Featuring in paddock photographer Kym Illman's 'Men of the Paddock' series brought another wave of new followers. It seemed as though each week there was something that would result in a comment asking who I was, which would be followed by lots of replies that included my '@F1Mech' Insta handle. This would again bring more followers.

I was still struggling with the whole idea, to be perfectly honest. I didn't particularly like the thought that I was getting all of this attention just because of my appearance. It wasn't something that I was used to and, in some ways, it created tensions in the garage with a couple of my teammates, who perhaps felt it was unfair that they weren't getting the same amount of recognition from the public. I felt similarly. Every single person in that garage deserves the same recognition for their talent and dedication. Everything that the team has achieved was only possible because all the people involved played their part. I wasn't comfortable making a name for myself based purely on the premise that I was the only Black guy in the race team, and one of the few Black men in the sport besides Sir Lewis Hamilton. After all, Lewis was one of the most successful race drivers that the world had ever seen, and I was just some guy who knew how to put a car together: we were not the same. It did feel unfair, but that wasn't something I could control. It didn't help that it had now become a running joke in the garage: 'Hollywood', 'Influencer' – these were some of the new nicknames I now had to endure. All in jest, of course, but slightly annoying nonetheless.

However, once I'd seen the opportunity to use my platform for good and started to engage with the public, I felt that the growth of that initial popularity was something I could earn, rather than feel like I was given. By offering insight into the sport that fans clearly wanted, I started to feel more comfortable with the idea that I could do some good, and that would always outweigh my pride.

It was partly my dad and one of my closest friends that helped to change my perspective on the whole situation. My dad said that being able to use a platform to inspire people is a fairly rare occurrence, and those who do find themselves in that situation should embrace it. It was a fitting comment from a man who had spent the latter part of his career helping others. As the first chief executive for Black and ethnic minority members of the Fire Brigades Union, something for which he was later awarded an MBE, my dad's opinions on these things would always leave a lasting impression.

My view now is that to be able to inspire those who share my love for the sport, but feel that they have little representation in the industry, is a responsibility. The people now messaging me had probably been trying to get the same information from the teams and other people in the paddock for ages, but to no avail. Or alternatively, they hadn't asked the questions at all because they didn't feel in any way connected to those that they saw involved in the sport. Who was I to ignore them? If it would only take a minute to answer somebody's question about career opportunities, or at least point them in the direction of resources, I felt like I had no excuse not to spare that minute.

Admittedly, nowadays, those messages come far too frequently to answer them all. This is why I try to find other ways to reach out to the public and offer this advice en masse.

It was this sense of responsibility that led me to being a guest on a podcast for the first time. *Driven by Diversity* was a podcast offering from the wonderful Ariana Bravo, who's now one of the fantastic presenters of Track TV, alongside the equally talented Steph Turner, who has gone on to have an inspiring career in communications in the Formula E paddock. Podcasts ultimately became one of my favourite mediums to reach people. That being my first, it probably wasn't my best, but seeing Ariana and Steph use the platform so well and then go on to have great careers means that it will always be my favourite.

It was some point around this time that a close friend, like my dad, also stepped in to tell me a truth that I needed to hear. . . I wasn't getting any younger and I didn't want to turn spanners for ever. He reminded me that if I let my pride stop me from taking an opportunity like the one that was presenting itself, I'd most likely regret it. Here I was with a chance to stay working in the industry that I love, but earn a living using my voice, my mind and an ever-growing social media presence, rather than punishing my body for thirty weeks a year. I would have had to be a total idiot not to try and embrace the potential for a change.

I have to say, though, it hasn't all been smooth sailing. Ultimately, the growth of my social media following, and my newfound willingness to embrace it and engage with people, would later put me at loggerheads with the very people who put me in the spotlight against my will to begin with: the team. The social media policy when I joined Red Bull Racing was incredibly restrictive, but it was also very basic and outdated. In many ways it contradicted itself to the point that working around it or ignoring it entirely was very easy. Nobody paid much attention back in 2018, unless you caused some sort of great scandal.

The team's social media policy was updated in 2022 and it's worth noting that, to this day I have still never signed and agreed to it. It is also fair to say that the team have never really pestered me to do so. For me, and the position I was in at the time the new policy was released, there were some inherent issues. The new policy essentially stated that if your profile mentioned that you worked at Red Bull Racing, then you had to ensure that your online presence was one that presented the company in a good light. That in itself was fine as none of the content on my socials could be seen as in any way controversial. The policy also stated that Red Bull wanted everyone to be an 'ambassador' for the team and take opportunities to highlight that Red Bull Racing was a great place to work. Again, I'd been promoting careers in the sport for a while and my online presence made it abundantly clear that I love what I do. Furthermore, Red Bull Racing *is* a great place to work, so it's not a particularly hard sell. Being an ambassador for the place you work isn't a challenge when you truly believe that your workplace is great, even if imperfect. I've always been extremely proud to represent an organisation that pushes the boundaries and has been pivotal in the growth of the sport in so many different aspects.

But as with anything in life, the situation was not perfect and this new social media policy did pose some problems for me with the surge in popularity I'd experienced on Instagram. The problem that I would later encounter was that it was now seemingly impossible for me to not be associated with Red Bull Racing. I don't mention them in my Instagram or Twitter bios any more and haven't for some time, but with *Drive to Survive* being instrumental at the beginning of my popularity growth, it was impossible for me to escape being associated with the team, and it wasn't long before tensions between me and some of the marketing and communications personnel began to run high.

It's easy to understand, from their perspective, why some people considered me to be a bit of a liability. I wasn't an official spokesperson for the company and therefore I hadn't received any media training. With my following on Instagram growing so quickly, it's safe to assume that there were worries from the marketing and communications departments that, at some point, I would say or do something that would get me in hot water and leave the team open to criticism. It would take a long time, but eventually I would gain the trust of most of these people. The others . . . I'm still working on.

The problem that I had with the new social media policy was essentially that there was a new one at all. Being able to ignore the previous policy because it was so outdated was perfect for me. The new document meant that people were now paying attention. So I decided that I'd ignore the request to sign the policy for a while, and wait to see if anyone ever came knocking, in the event of which I'd plead ignorance. Despite getting a few reminders from HR via Workday, nobody has ever actually come to ask why I have not signed the new policy, or any team document that refers to it, since 2021.

There were a few clauses in particular that I simply couldn't accept. The first of these was that, unless signed off by management, we were not permitted to do interviews in any form. This ruled out doing podcasts, which I was really starting to enjoy and were also giving me great feedback. I'd also made it clear to the team that it was a great way to reach underrepresented groups and inspire them to get involved in motorsport. Informal conversations and personal stories were far more effective at providing insight than corporate language and seemingly forced initiatives. This new policy was also an issue for me as I'd recorded two podcasts just the week before it was sent out, and they were due to be released later that month.

Another problem was that the new social media policy also specifically stated that we shouldn't do Q & As in any form, something that I had done with great success with my followers on Instagram just a month or so prior. I couldn't help but think that this rule was a little bit personal. I knew that when I had done the Q & A previously, it had rubbed a few of our comms personnel up the wrong way.

Finally, the new social media policy explicitly told us that 'sponsored' or 'paid' work on social media was forbidden, something that I had been engaged in already. It was over this policy that I had my first direct conflict with the team's marketing department, something that had been brewing for some time, and I had already decided that I wouldn't be browbeaten over it. Ultimately my stance on this was very simple. While I was very proud to be an employee of Red Bull Racing, I was not the property of Red Bull Racing. Other than relating to things that had the potential to bring the company into disrepute, I felt that the team should have no right to tell me what I could and couldn't do with my time outside of work (the exception to this being working for a competitor, as outlined in my contract). I knew that I had a contractual duty to inform human resources of any outside interest that could be considered a conflict, but that was it.

By the start of 2023, I had enlisted the help of an amazing manager in Francesca Scambler, who, while growing her new agency, District Global, had been working tirelessly to find opportunities for me to earn outside of the racetrack and use my ever-growing following to my advantage. As well as public speaking engagements, there were plenty of businesses hopeful of reaching my audience. One such company was White Claw, an American alcoholic drinks company that makes 'hard seltzer'. They had approached Francesca and invited me to the British Summer Time Festival in Hyde Park. It was all very simple: they had asked me to attend the event, spend the day capturing the atmosphere at the festival and include their product as a main feature in some content on my Instagram page. For this they would pay me a fee and cover all expenses. White Claw wasn't the first drinks brand that had approached me to do this kind of work, but I had been careful not to work with any brands that could be considered in conflict with Red Bull. As far I was concerned, as White Claw was an alcoholic beverage, there was no conflict, and so I agreed.

The content went live towards the end of the summer shutdown period in 2023 and was well received. The content itself was very inoffensive in nature: a 'reel' of my partner and me having a nice day out at a festival, enjoying some drinks and live music. Due to advertising law in the UK, as I had been paid to create the content and post it, I had to apply the 'paid partnership' tag to it on Instagram. This was where things got difficult because, in doing so, I was in direct conflict with the new Red Bull Racing social media policy, which I still hadn't signed more than a year after its release. I heard nothing from anyone at Red Bull for a week or so after the content was posted, but my gut told me that a storm was brewing.

When we returned to work after the summer break, just before we flew out to the Austrian Grand Prix, many of my race team colleagues approached me to ask if I had experienced any backlash to my apparent flouting of the new rules. I said that although I hadn't yet, I knew it was coming.

Coincidently, Francesca had been approached that week by a charity called the Renaissance Foundation, which works to improve the lives of young carers and patients. They had been taking young people to the Silverstone Grand Prix for many years and had asked if I would be willing to find some time on the Thursday prior to the race to talk to their group about what I did, how I got there and, if possible, give a short tour of the garage. Of course, this was exactly the kind of thing that I wanted to do. It's the reason I had embraced my newfound platform. To this day, I will always try and find time to support these kinds of initiatives, and it's now become one of my favourite parts of the job.

As I would be appearing in team kit and at the racetrack, I knew that I would be viewed as an ambassador of the company and therefore I needed to seek permission to do so. I also knew that this would essentially be a formality: there was no way that Red Bull would reject this request from a charity. So, I sent an email to Jonathan Wheatley, who was still the team's sporting director at the time, the head of marketing and also one of the comms leads. The email outlined the request and ended with something like 'Does anybody have any objections to this?'

Jonathan Wheatley's response was swift. He had no objections, thought it was a great initiative and said that he was confident that I wouldn't allow this to affect my ability to manage my workload that week. It has to be said that Jonathan was always a great supporter of mine, both in my professional career and in my work promoting diversity and inclusion in the industry. He was one of the few senior managers in the paddock that genuinely seemed as though he recognised the issues, and he had wanted to see a more diverse paddock for a long time.

Marketing, too, had no issues with me speaking with a charity group, and only commented to say that if there was anything else I required, I need just ask.

The final reply to my request came a few days later, once I had already arrived in Austria. While the comms lead didn't have any outright objections to my request, the email ended with 'I also need to grab a few minutes to talk with you about something else at some point this week'. I knew, of course, what this 'something else' was going to be. It was definitely going to be about my 'paid partnership' post with White Claw.

The Saturday evening prior to the Austrian Grand Prix, I received a text message from one of the team's marketing personnel. He asked if I had a few minutes for 'a chat' the following morning prior to the race. He is a nice guy; I like him, and we've got on well over the years. I almost felt bad for him that it seemed he'd been put up to the task of trying to challenge me about the White Claw content on my Instagram. I had already discussed with my partner that I wasn't going to kowtow to the team on this matter. I had decided that while I was extremely proud to represent the team, my personal social media was where I would draw the line on interference in my life. While I accepted that I had a responsibility never to bring the team into disrepute,

I also felt that they had no right to tell me how I leveraged my following for my benefit.

The conversation that unfolded on the Sunday morning prior to the Austrian Grand Prix was the first time I had ever really clashed with the team about anything in the ten years I'd been a part of it. When one of the team's marketing staff was given the task of challenging me about the White Claw post, I think he expected me to just say, 'Sorry, I won't do it again'. But by the time I walked away from the conversation, leaving him standing by the side of one of our race trucks, he was speechless. He seemed totally unprepared for my rigid stance on this matter. The conversation was calm and civil, all the way up until he made the mistake of saying (in an incredibly condescending tone), 'Calum, you only have your platform because you work for the team'.

This statement was like a red rag to a bull for me. Bearing in mind that this was three years after I first started to gain popularity on social media, the insinuation that I deserved none of the credit for the growth of my own profile was unacceptable in my view. Although I knew that this tended to be the view of many in the marketing department, to express it in so dismissive a way pissed me off. Their view ignored both the effort I'd been putting in to engage with the public and the overwhelmingly positive responses, which were obviously beneficial to the team. The opinion that he expressed wasn't fair or appropriate in my eyes, and so I responded assertively.

'Well, if we're being really honest here, I have my platform because both yourselves and Netflix decided to leverage my ethnicity to make the team appear to the public as more ethnically diverse. Furthermore, if the company wants to try and take all the credit for my social media following, are you also prepared to take responsibility for the daily racial abuse I receive? I know that you are aware of it. You can't have it both ways, so which is it?'

After I'd finished, there was a painfully long silence. Like I said, I felt quite bad for him; he is a nice guy and it was clear to me that he'd been put up to this. He stuttered for a while and then changed his tone entirely when he eventually responded: 'I just wanted to discuss it with you before it ended up on Christian Horner's desk. I just don't want you to get in trouble . . . perhaps there are some tools we can give you to help with the abuse.'

I told him to keep his tools and stay out of my personal affairs. I also said that if Christian wanted to have this conversation in person, I was more than happy to do so. Politics runs through all aspects of the paddock, not just the sporting bits. I knew damn well that Christian did not have the time or inclination to be worrying about what I was posting on my Instagram, and it was a ridiculous thing to suggest as much. It was at this point that I just walked off and went for breakfast.

It wasn't an ideal start to a Sunday morning, but I actually felt relieved to have put my cards on the table and make it clear that I wouldn't be bullied on this matter.

About twenty minutes later, while eating, I watched from across the Red Bull Energy Station – the team's regular private hospitality space – as a conversation between the marketing guy and a trackside comms representative unfolded. I pointed them out to a colleague I was sitting with, having just explained to them what had occurred. I must admit, I enjoyed watching the comms lead's disappointed face and shaking head as it was explained how the conversation had gone. The shrugging of the shoulders also told me all I needed to know: they weren't going to challenge me on the subject further.

Since then, my relationship with marketing and comms has actually been great. Sometimes a bit more honesty and a little less posturing works wonders for everyone. Marketing and comms seem to be the two areas of the business that have the highest turnover of staff, a trend seen in a lot of businesses. It was frustrating for me, though. Every time I'd started to build a relationship with comms about my social media activity, the person in charge seemed to change. Finally, things on this front started to improve in 2023 after the team took on a new trackside head of communications, Paul Smith. Paul was a breath of fresh air. I've never met anyone in comms as brutally honest and straight-talking with me. I knew we'd get on well almost immediately.

I also had a good relationship with Victoria Lloyd, the head of internal communications in Milton Keynes. I had known and worked alongside Vicky back at Status GP right at the very beginning of my career. She had always been great and when she had been trackside at Red Bull Racing, I never hesitated to approach her regarding things that I wanted to do. She later became pivotal in helping to publicise the team's diversity and inclusion strategies, so I was regularly in contact with her about various things I was doing in relation to that.

Paul joined the team in 2022 and I hadn't known him for very long when I wondered whether we might clash for the first time. By the time he joined the team, I had already started enacting my policy of not asking permission, something that was pissing off some of the other communications staff. I quickly learned that not only was Paul very open and easy to deal with, but he seemed supportive of anything that I wanted to do provided it wasn't detrimental to the team. He also seemed to come with no ego whatsoever, which was refreshing, and when we did talk, he was happy to be perfectly honest about where he and others stood on any particular matter. Over the 2023 US Grand Prix weekend in Austin, Texas, I was to experience this refreshing honesty first hand.

Francesca had arranged for me to do an appearance on Sky Sports News one morning, in the week between the Qatar and United States Grand Prix. It was a huge opportunity for me. Sky Sports News wanted some insight into what it was like to work with both such a successful team, as Red Bull Racing were fresh off the back of winning the World Constructors' Championship in dominant fashion, and such a successful driver, as Max Verstappen had just secured his third World Drivers' Championship in the most successful season that the sport had ever seen.

Most importantly for me, Sky had given me the chance to steer the conversation towards any other topics that I felt were important. Naturally, I said that I wanted to talk about diversity and inclusion in the industry, and how we can improve the opportunities for all and remove some of the barriers that underrepresented groups had faced. I recognised that this was a big opportunity for me and, although it was only an eight-minute slot, I was, of course, a bit nervous. This was partly because it would be the first time that I'd have done any kind of live interview, and I was acutely aware that there was no chance to edit or fix any errors. I was also nervous because, as per my own new policy, I hadn't sought any kind of permission from Red Bull Racing, or even mentioned it. This second worry became even more nerve-wracking when Sky suggested that, while I was there, I could also do an episode of their F1 podcast with Matt Baker as well as doing a fan Q & A for their other social channels. All three of these things flew directly in the face of the still unsigned social media policy at Red Bull.

I said to Phoebe on the way out of the door in the morning that this could be the day that helped me change the course of my career or the day that got me fired. She joked that if I did get fired, it would probably just help me to sell this book. My retort was that the book might not pay the mortgage and, at that point in time, it was a long way from being finished.

Thankfully, that morning at Sky went better than I could have ever expected. The live interview went so well that I was completely relaxed by the time we were recording the podcast and Q & A, and as such they were hugely successful. Matt Baker is a brilliant host, and that podcast is one of my favourites to date. Most of all, I was just relieved that I didn't shit myself when the cameras went live, or accidently say something that people could deliberately misinterpret to sound in some way controversial.

Once it was done, I spent the next few days keeping tabs on the public reaction across the various social media channels. I thought that if the overall reaction was positive, then even if the communications team were unhappy that I'd done the interviews without permission, they wouldn't have any grounds to reprimand me. I figured that I would be the last of the comms team's worries, provided that it went well.

The public reaction was, once again, hugely positive. There was a lot of engagement across the various channels, with very few negative comments, and those that were negative were all from people that had simply decided they didn't like me because of my choice of employer or because I didn't work for their favourite driver. I could live with that.

I flew to Austin confident that I wouldn't get in too much trouble, despite my blatant disregard for the company's rules. When half of the comments read 'I hate Red Bull, except this guy' or 'This guy is the only good thing about that team', I guess it became apparent that disciplining me for breaking the rules would have made absolutely no sense. I think there were a few grumbles from some members of the comms team that I'd kept the interview to myself and not sought permission before agreeing to it but as I've said, at that point, asking for forgiveness rather than permission had become my default. In this instance (and to my own disbelief) I didn't even have to ask for forgiveness.

I ran into Paul in the paddock in Austin, and he stopped me and asked to have a word. I remember thinking, *Here we go, time for my insincere apology.* I couldn't have been more wrong.

'Cal, I just wanted to say that I saw your podcast on Sky Sports and I thought it was fantastic. I've sent it over for Christian to watch. I think we should be finding ways to support you doing this stuff because I think it's great, people clearly love it and you're very good at it.'

I was stunned. At best, I was hoping that the team might just decide to ignore it; at worst, I was expecting a bollocking. I certainly wasn't expecting praise for my performance and an offer of support to do more in the way of media work. So, imagine my surprise when later that afternoon I walked past the hospitality unit and, through the glass windows, I could see Christian Horner and Jonathan Wheatley watching me on the *Sky Sports F1 Podcast.*

I walked back into the garage with a smug grin on my face and thought to myself, *I wish I had the time to sit around watching a podcast on Thursday afternoon at a race weekend. Oh, how the other half live!*

CHAPTER 9

The Push to Diversify

Even before I had embarked on my career in motorsport, before I had even enrolled at college, something that was apparently obvious to my peers was brought to my attention. I remember clearly returning from the Silverstone Grand Prix in 2009 and having various conversations with different friends where I would tell them that I had decided that this was what I was going to do for a living: that I was going to be a race mechanic and ultimately the goal was Formula One.

There were two very distinct and different reactions to this announcement. The first, usually from my white friends – the people with whom I had gone to school and actually spent most of my time – was one of excitement and encouragement. I don't get a lot of time to catch up with these friends now but, when I do, usually over the Christmas period, I let them know that I'm eternally grateful for their support and encouragement back when it was hard for me to come by. They knew that it would be an environment I would thrive in – they'd seen my competitive nature first hand when we were playing sport during our school days. Ultimately, they were right: I would go on to thrive in an industry that allowed me to play to my strengths.

The response to my plans from my Black friends and cousins was almost entirely different. While they were obviously supportive of all of my endeavours, there was almost a sense of confusion and bewilderment. I remember feeling, in some cases, that I'd disappointed them for deciding to pursue a career that traditionally wasn't seen as a place for Black men. Later on, while I was at college, one of my friends just said outright, 'But, Cal, that's a white man's game. They ain't gonna let you in.'

It's worth mentioning at this point that I'm extremely proud of my mixed heritage. Having a white British mother and Black British-Caribbean father has afforded me the privilege of being able to see some complicated issues surrounding ethnicity from multiple viewpoints. To the outside world, most mixed-heritage people will have spent their lives being viewed by the world as Black, or at least non-white. I'm sure I'm not the first person to have felt at times that they were too Black for the white kids but not Black enough for the Black kids. Certainly, when I was younger, I always felt some level of guilt that I wasn't

THE PUSH TO DIVERSIFY

nearly as connected to my Caribbean heritage as some of my cousins. Later on in my career, my decision to grow my dreadlocks was partly one that I took as a daily reminder and expression of my Caribbean heritage, a tribute to where a huge part of what made me came from. As an adult, I haven't found nearly enough time to go to Dominica and spend time with my grandparents. I do look forward to taking my daughter there and letting her experience what a wonderful culture it has.

That statement that one of my Black friends made about being 'let in' was something that stuck with me for a long time, and at different points in my career it impacted the way that I thought about the industry and my own prospects. My hair is a great example of this. I'd wanted to grow my hair since I was a kid but my parents never let me. This was because they understood that society is inherently biased against traditionally Black hairstyles, and this is something that I'm still aware of today. When I joined the sport, there were still Formula One teams that wouldn't hire people with tattoos or beards, so I can't imagine that dreadlocks would have been a recipe for success. There's no doubt in my mind that had I arrived for interviews in motorsport with dreadlocks back in 2009, despite any amount of skill and dedication, my career would be non-existent – it's a sad reality.

I didn't have the confidence to finally grow my hair until I'd been comfortable in my job at Red Bull Racing for many years and, therefore, I felt it was less likely to evoke the implicit biases that Caribbean hairstyles often do. It's also fair to say that the nature of Red Bull Racing as an organisation is in some part the reason I had the confidence to grow it.

I still think about it now, though. If I were to want to move into executive management at a race team, I'd probably consider cutting off my dreads. Not because a hairstyle has any bearing on my ability or what I might offer to the job role, but because I don't think I would be considered for the job or taken seriously with dreadlocks – not by enough people who mattered anyway. While I'm very proud to be able to provide some representation to those who are beginning their careers now, there's still really nobody for me to look up to in that sense. Like so many sports, senior management throughout Formula One represents a very narrow demographic. Since losing Claire Williams as the only female deputy team principal in 2020, the sport's upper management is certainly lagging behind the rest of the industry in terms of diversity. While this is true of most major sports, even those where the vast majority of the athletes are Black, like the NBA, it's particularly noticeable in Formula One.

It wasn't until much later in my career that the gravity of my friend's 'they ain't gonna let you in' view really hit home. It wasn't that he wasn't supportive of my goals, it was that it simply seemed absurd to him, a working-class Black man, that Formula One was a realistic goal for someone who looked like us. Lewis Hamilton had just won his first

Formula One world championship in 2008, but he and his father Anthony were the only Black men that most people had seen involved in the sport in any way. What Black people in the UK had also seen in the news was that, recently, Lewis had been racially abused by fans in Barcelona.

At the time, I was quite annoyed at my friend for holding the view that any success would be unlikely just because of our skin colour, but when I look back I accept that, actually, it was a valid opinion based on the information that he had available to him. While, for many, this kind of comment may have dissuaded them from making any attempt to pursue a career in the industry, it only fuelled me further to prove him wrong.

Representation matters. We often hear this phrase now, but I'm not sure I fully understood the impact of representation before I became a part of providing some for young Black engineers like myself. When I look back to the beginning of my career, I wonder if I would have discovered the industry I love sooner, had there been anyone to look to for inspiration. Really, I only discovered that there were amazing career opportunities in motorsport by chance, because a friend of a friend was doing Formula Two and had told me about the National College for Motorsport at Silverstone. Without this tenuous link to somebody already working in the industry, my life would probably look very different now.

Before Liberty's takeover from Bernie Ecclestone and the subsequent Netflix docuseries, there really was no exposure for those working behind the scenes. The sport was so closed off from engaging new audiences that the vast majority of those working in the industry were following a long line of family members who had already been involved in it in some way. As I've said, during my time in college, I was one of the few students who had absolutely no experience of professional racing. Most of the other students had some connection to motorsport, whether through a dad, an uncle or suchlike. In terms of representation for me at the time, there was none.

This meant that there were two things I would have to deal with right from the beginning. The first was that I was going to stick out like a sore thumb; it was unavoidable. When you work in a sport where you are the only Black person in an entire pitlane, you stand out. For at least a little while longer, if you are a Black person aiming to work in European motorsport, you'll need to get used to that.

The second is that, if you find yourself as the only Black person in a team or business, it's going to be thrust upon you at some point to answer questions that people feel they need a Black opinion on. Nowadays, among my teammates at Red Bull, I'm happy to answer people's questions and share what I've learned over the years about barriers to entry in motorsport. In the garage, we have all manner of debates and discussions on topics relating to diversity in the sport. I try and create an environment where my colleagues are comfortable asking me often difficult questions. Older and wiser, I can now respond to some of those questions but, when I was only twenty-one, I simply didn't have the answers. I hadn't been able to learn from other Black people in the sport, and therefore I didn't have the confidence to have those difficult conversations.

'Cal, how come you're the only Black guy?'

'Why don't Black people care about racing?'

I just couldn't answer those types of questions from my colleagues early in my career, and I'd often feel awkward or ashamed at not having the answers people were looking for. It would take me a decade of understanding the industry and the issues before I was ready but, as the only Black mechanic anyone in the team had ever worked with, I was somehow expected to know all this stuff already. It was difficult enough to try to respond to the questions at all, but to do so without upsetting anyone or making them feel like I was personally blaming them was almost impossible.

On top of that, my friend's 'they ain't gonna let you in' comment was still firmly implanted in my mind. I worried that if I was too honest about the barriers Black people face, or too outspoken about injustices certain groups face throughout society, then perhaps it would hinder my career progress. I didn't want to get kicked out of the circle now that they had 'let me in'.

For years, because of these fears, whenever I was drawn into such conversations, I'd stop short of being completely honest with my colleagues. I'd just sort of allude to the fact that they and I weren't playing to the same set of rules and we weren't held to the same standards, without going into too much detail. It wasn't particularly helpful for them, nor was it healthy for me. I often used to drive back down the M1 on my way home and have those conversations over and over again in my head, thinking about all the things I should have said.

I'd love to be able tell you that in my fifteen years of racing I've never been subjected to any incidents of racism, either overt or systemic. Yes, I'd love to tell you that, but it would be a lie. The truth is that early on there were plenty. Even during my time at college, when I was trying to find work experience in the Britcar paddock, it already seemed as though I was going into an industry where I'd be at a disadvantage to my peers because of the way I looked. Some of the experiences I had, the things I saw and heard, would likely never happen in a race team today. If they did, they would certainly not be tolerated, but I felt obliged to tolerate them back then.

Weirdly, my first real experience of overt racism in the workplace is one that I now consider to have had a positive impact on my confidence, especially in relation to the need to speak up when you know something is wrong. At the time, I was appalled that someone I had been working alongside had felt it appropriate to behave in such a manner. When I look back on it, the thing that I'm reminded of is that there are far more good people in this industry than bad, and that is something that is trending in the right direction as a new, more tolerant generation begins to lead the industry forward.

The way in which this first experience came about is surprisingly also rather amusing. All the way back in 2010, when I was doing GP3, Le Mans and some other work as it came along with various teams, trying to build my CV, one of the teams I was working for had a contractor that used to come in to do gearbox work. He was an older white British man who seemed to have pissed off all the other mechanics with some of his working practices. Mess, lost tools, dirty equipment . . . these are all ways to make enemies in a race workshop and this guy was a repeat offender. As a result of this, the other mechanics had started playing some rather annoying but usually innocuous practical jokes on him. Simple things like sawing half an inch off of one leg of the stool he always sat on so that it wobbled, or using lockwire to keep equipment attached to the benches it was supposed to live on. It really wasn't anything harmful but, yes, it was very annoying for him.

At this point in my career, I wasn't in a position to be playing pranks on people, so I was just an observer. On top of that, this person was a seasoned technician, so someone with a supposedly expert skillset who I wanted to learn from, rather than upset. However, despite being told repeatedly by others that I had nothing to do with it, this guy was convinced that I was the one playing these practical jokes.

One day, the other mechanics probably went a bit too far. The contractor had spent most of the day fitting studs into brand new gearbox casings in preparation for the ELMS season. The process involved cleaning out the freshly machined holes and threads with brake cleaner, applying Loctite to the threads, and then tightening the studs into the holes to the specified torque. After about five or six hours, with many gearboxes completed, the contractor realised that someone had swapped the contents of the brake-cleaner bottle for water and Fairy Liquid. I distinctly remember, when one of the mechanics told me what they'd done, asking how he'd not noticed the different smell yet. I wasn't sure how he could not have noticed that the usually pungent solvent suddenly smelled like wild-rose washing-up liquid.

When he did finally realise what had happened and the amount of work that would now need to be redone, he absolutely lost it. I wasn't present for what happened next, as I'd gone home for the evening. When I got to the workshop the following morning, one of the chief mechanics asked to grab a word with me.

Now, the reason I consider this incident to have ultimately had a positive impact on me is because of what happened that morning in the chief mechanics' office. When I'd been called into the office, my first assumption was that I was in trouble. Perhaps it was a mental hangover from my time in school where I spent most mornings being interrogated over some incident or another, but what he said next stunned me into an uncharacteristic silence.

The chief mechanic told me that, the previous evening, our gearbox contractor had stormed into the office to complain about the practical jokes that had been going on and pointed the finger at me. I tried to interrupt and explain that I hadn't been the one playing pranks, but he stopped me . . . he already knew. So, he continued and explained that before he'd had the chance to correct the guy and explain to him that I wasn't the one responsible, the technician had used a racial slur about me during his rant. The chief mechanic awkwardly recounted what was said, including the racial slur. It wasn't an easy moment for either of us, and there was an uncomfortable silence before he continued. It was the first time that I'd had to deal with overt discrimination in a professional setting, so I didn't really know how I was supposed to react. The chief mechanic went on to explain that as well as informing the gearbox technician that I wasn't the one who'd been messing with him, he had also told him that the language used was unacceptable and did not align with the values of the team. Therefore his services would no longer be required.

It was an unexpected start to my day, to say the least. I've always felt that it's far easier for a manager to take action against something that happens publicly, as opposed to an incident that occurs behind closed doors. In a public setting, they really have no choice in the modern workplace: if everyone has heard a racial slur being used, a manager knows they have to do something about it or face repercussions themselves. What is said in a private office, however, is far easier to overlook. Taking action in those circumstances is a test of conscience. Knowing that this chief mechanic took action simply because he knew right from wrong, and his values aligned with mine, was one of the most significant boosts to my confidence in my entire career. He had chosen to do right, despite the inconvenience it would cause him. His decision to take immediate action let me know that I was a valued member of that team, even if I was just a junior at the time.

This story is an important reminder that even if you feel alone (as I often did at the time), the majority of people you will work alongside will be more welcoming, understanding and interested in your welfare than you might imagine. I've always felt that in motorsport, particularly in Formula One, many people have spent their lives travelling the world, seeing and experiencing different cultures, so they should be best placed to create an inclusive community. I haven't, for a long time, felt that sport's biggest barriers lie with overt prejudice or a wilfully ignorant culture. Rather, at least over the last five years, we've seen meaningful change in that regard, and certainly in terms of how Black mechanics are viewed.

Since Sir Lewis Hamilton sparked the long overdue public conversation about why the sport was so lacking in diversity, attitudes and practices in general have shifted. When racing resumed after COVID in 2020, and with the public still reeling from the footage of George Floyd's murder at the hands of a US law enforcement officer in May of that year, Lewis used his status as one of the greatest athletes in history to highlight the injustices that many Black people still face around the world. When he later launched the Hamilton Commission, Lewis aimed to highlight the barriers to opportunity that make STEM careers inaccessible for some. This sparked a long-overdue public conversation. People were finally asking why motorsport had fallen so far behind the rest of the sporting world in terms of the diversity of those working in it, and what that said about the inclusivity of the businesses operating in the industry. Founding the Hamilton Commission and pledging money and resources for independent research to highlight the barriers to entry into the sport was the beginning of a shift in how Formula One teams approached inclusion in their workplaces.

I'm glad to say that some of the things that I saw and heard early on in my career would simply never happen now. Fifteen years on from my own bad experiences, many of my colleagues now understand some of the reasons that people from ethnic minorities are underrepresented in engineering, and in time many more will have an interest in helping to break down those barriers to opportunity.

It can be difficult being one of very few Black people working in any workplace. For one thing, as I've touched upon, you'll often be expected to share your opinion on any ethnicity-related talking points in the news, but also not offend anyone with your views. Either that, or you'll become acutely aware that your colleagues don't seem to talk freely whenever you're around, or while having a post-race beer in the hotel lobby, for fear they might offend you.

If you are planning on embarking on a motorsport career as a person who is Black, Asian or from another ethnic minority, then my advice with regard to talking to people about issues surrounding sensitive subjects such as ethnicity or religion is to be prepared to hear things that might offend some. My policy with my colleagues during my time in racing has always been simple – if we're having any kind of interaction, professional or otherwise, then they should never be afraid of offending me unless it was their intention to do so. Intent is everything. The reason that I say this is because if people are terrified of using an incorrect term or phrasing something poorly without intending to offend, then often conversation is shut down entirely. If no conversation can be had, then no progress can be made.

As an example, anytime Paul Bellringer would refer to a Black man when telling me a story, he would use the phrase 'coloured lad'. Jokingly, I would respond with 'What colour was he, Paul?' He would immediately know what I was getting at, apologise, and then tentatively say 'a Black guy'. I was never offended at the use of a term we now frown upon because, firstly, Paul's intention was never to offend; secondly, I used to quite enjoy winding Paul up a bit when he realised his mistake; and thirdly, I recognise that Paul's generation was taught that 'coloured' was the inoffensive term to use. I get that old habits die hard. I sometimes find it difficult myself. When speaking as a panellist at a Red Bull Racing event for International Women in Engineering Day in 2024, I had to concentrate extremely hard to not say things like 'Hi, guys'. I did a training session where someone suggested that, instead, we should say 'Hi, everyone', but it's easier said than done. One person suggested saying 'Hi, friends'. I couldn't see that one catching on, to be honest.

Most workplaces simply tell colleagues not to discuss things like politics, religion or anything that they would refer to as a 'potentially sensitive subject' while at work, in order to avoid this kind of potential conflict. But what use is that, really? How can we expect to change attitudes and find common ground without discussion? My colleagues at Red Bull know that even if they were to phrase something badly or use a term that people could find offensive, it wasn't likely that I was going to make any formal complaint to HR. At worst, I would feel the need to interject and explain why I felt something was inappropriate.

I understand that it's very easy for me to say all this now, having spent over a decade in the paddock and experiencing the relative comfort, status and confidence that comes with it. I don't pretend for one minute that back in 2012 I would have been as self-assured or felt supported enough to have had this attitude. My hope going forward is that those embarking on careers in motorsport now will naturally see more diverse workplaces throughout the industry. If that is the case, it won't be because we never talked about anything. It will be the result of the many voices within the sport that were crying out to have these conversations, me being one of them.

The launch of the Hamilton Commission and its report into diversity and inclusion throughout UK motorsport was the first time since embarking on a career in racing that I'd had any official platform to discuss the barriers that many face in pursuit of engineering careers.

From the first time I sat down with Lewis to discuss the commission and its goals, it was immediately clear how passionate he was about making change. Outside the Mercedes hospitality suite in Abu Dhabi in 2020, Zimbabwean-born chemical engineer Stephanie Travers and I sat with Lewis and shared our thoughts on some of the barriers to opportunity for those from underrepresented backgrounds. We identified some areas that we felt could be addressed, and I spoke at length about how I felt provision for apprenticeships was key to training the next generation of mechanics and technicians. I'll always be an advocate for creating these opportunities, not just in Formula One, but throughout racing in all its guises. Provision for allowing people to earn while learning is a huge stepping stone.

This short chat on a Saturday evening at a racetrack – at the beginning of a long-overdue conversation that Lewis would force the industry to have – was inspiring. Seeing Lewis so passionate about ensuring that he would leave behind a better sport than the one he joined lit a fire. Having one of the sport's greats use his platform for the good of future generations was an incredible thing, and I felt honoured that Lewis had asked me to participate in his task. It excited me to an extent that I hadn't felt since that first pitlane walk in 2009.

I accepted an invitation to provide a case study for the researchers putting together the commission report, speaking about my experiences and how I felt about the environments I'd worked in. Being asked to do this formally for the first time made me realise that, other than my own experiences, I actually knew very little about the different barriers people face trying to access motorsport. While I obviously knew my own journey so far, it took me a while to identify and understand exactly what barriers I'd overcome already. I just hadn't thought about my own story in that way. As with the rest of the sport, I'm still learning these things now.

In my view, the Hamilton Commission report did two very important things for the sport of Formula One and for the teams that compete in it. The first was to provide reliable data about the people who were involved in the sport and those who were studying areas relevant to the sector. At the time Lewis first commissioned this research, to be undertaken independently by the Royal Academy of Engineering, not all the teams even had this data available to them. As a member of one the working groups that look at diversity and inclusion at Red Bull Racing, I asked in one of the first meetings why we'd been unable to provide this information about our workforce to the commission. It seems absurd to me that businesses that rely so desperately on accurate data when competing on the track had almost no information about the people that made up their workforce. Without knowing where we stood at that time, how was the sport supposed to collectively make lasting change? And how would we know if anything that we did was working?

The answer as to why there was no information was that, for many years, businesses in the UK were almost taught not to ask these things. This was because personal information on criteria such as ethnicity, gender or sexuality could have been used to discriminate during the application process, which has been a genuine concern for many in the UK for decades. The end result of this, though, was that most teams had very little personal information about their staff at all. As a data engineer would say, there was no baseline.

The Hamilton commission made teams wake up and take note. Pretty much all of the teams in the Formula One paddock now know more about the people that make up their workforce. Crucially, this gives them the vital data required to understand which groups are underrepresented in their business. This is key to understanding the different barriers that exist to entry into the sport. Only when we can understand these barriers, and how they affect different groups in different ways, are we then able to look at ways to break those barriers down and provide more equity in a company's practices and better opportunity to those who could potentially be the engineers of the future.

For me, the second and most important thing that the Hamilton Commission did was start a conversation. For years, people like me and others in the sport from underrepresented groups could see many of the issues, but we simply had no voice. At least, not a voice that needed to be listened to. Lewis leveraged his profile at great personal risk in order to help make change happen, and inspired plenty of people as a result.

There are now lots of organisations devoted to engaging people in STEM that didn't exist previously. When I was starting out there were none at all. Mission 44, a direct result of Lewis's efforts, works to create a more inclusive education system and provide employment opportunities in STEM. Motivez, founded by Driven By Us member George Imafidon MBE, is doing some incredible work engaging young people in STEM in some of the UK's most underserved communities. All of these are great resources if you want to begin a career in racing, and I wish that they had been available to me when I needed them most.

Once I started to take note of the issues myself, something that I hadn't done early on in my career, it became very apparent to me that the barriers for different groups varied hugely. While I've often felt that many of the systemic issues in motorsport tend to reflect those of society in general, I also feel that there are areas where we've made good progress. I do think, however, that there are some areas where motorsport has fallen behind the curve in terms of making workplaces more inclusive.

Understandably, I tend to use my own experiences as examples and then go on to try and learn about the experiences of others. My own experiences of racism earlier on in my career gave me a perfectly good understanding of the implicit bias that many Black people face when embarking on careers in racing but, admittedly, until I met my partner, I hadn't paid enough attention to how those same biases affected women in the sport.

I met Phoebe at the beginning of the 2014 season while I was working for Marussia F1. Phoebe worked for a catering and hospitality company, a contractor to Marussia. The first chance we had to spend any real time together was one evening in Shanghai, China, when we went out in a large group to a popular paddock haunt called Mint. Phoebe and I hit it off that night and I guess the rest is history, as they say.

At the time, something that I had never really considered was that women in the paddock were (and, in my opinion, still are) held to a completely different standard and expected to behave completely differently from the men working in the sport. What Phoebe had kept from me for the first few weeks that we'd been dating was that she had concerns that, should our relationship become public knowledge, she would lose her job. I was completely oblivious that this had been bothering her until she finally shared it with me. The reason for this was because, in my experience, any mechanic that went on a night out and successfully 'pulled' would be lauded by his colleagues in the garage the following day. This simply isn't the case for the women working in a male-dominated sport. It turned out that Phoebe's employer, as with so many at the time, had a reputation for dismissing any woman who was found to have been sleeping with a mechanic from the paddock. It was, and often still is, a grossly unfair double standard.

The first time we were out together while away at a race, we were spotted by one of my colleagues from the garage, and Phoebe was instantly on edge. Having been made aware of the issues by Phoebe, the next day I made an effort to go and see this colleague and impress on him the importance of keeping the information to himself. Thankfully he did and we managed to keep the nature of our relationship a closely guarded secret for another few months.

It wasn't until later in the year, at the Canadian Grand Prix, that Phoebe's boss discovered our relationship. We were out for dinner at the Keg, a popular steak restaurant in the old French district of Montreal. Towards the end of our meal, the waitress brought two strawberry daquiris over to the table and when Phoebe tried to explain that we hadn't ordered them, the waitress said that they'd been purchased by someone across the other side of the restaurant and sent over to us. As we looked over to where the waitress was pointing, the realisation set in that, sitting at the table, was Phoebe's boss.

Now, those familiar with Montreal will know that there are two Keg restaurants in the downtown area, and Phoebe and I had deliberately chosen the quieter of the two in the hope of this not happening, such was our worry about being discovered. It is worth noting that by this point most of my colleagues were aware that we'd been dating, and nobody had even batted an eyelid, other than the few that cared enough to warn us about keeping our relationship a secret for her sake.

Phoebe's employer, however, had since dismissed at least two other members of his hospitality staff since the beginning of our relationship, apparently for the same heinous crime of being involved with mechanics. Oddly, this was probably the only reason why Phoebe wasn't punished. Quite simply, her boss couldn't afford to lose any more staff. Even so, the arrival of those strawberry daquiris was the start of a few tense days as Phoebe waited to see how her employer would handle it.

I think that it's fair to say that discrimination is something that women in the sport, particularly those who choose technical pathways, still have to deal with to a much greater extent than those from Black and ethnic minority communities. Certainly, when I think about my own experience, it's been over a decade since I felt that I was being treated poorly or spoken to inappropriately due to my ethnicity. However, when I speak to some of the women that I've worked with over the years and hear some of their experiences, it's quite shocking to learn some of the things they've had to deal with (and in many cases are still dealing with) during the course of their careers. Inappropriate language and behaviour, or unsolicited advice that's only given to the women in the team, are just some of the things that I have been told about. Once you hear these things and get a picture of the environment many women still face in motorsport, you start to understand why women are still so underrepresented in technical roles.

As far as I'm aware, there's no scientific study that suggests women are less able or naturally talented in STEM disciplines. There are also plenty of talented women who study and graduate with the qualifications to take on these technical roles in motorsport. What the data from the Hamilton Commission report suggests to me is that many women make a conscious choice not to take their relevant skills into motorsport careers. I get the impression that many of these women can surmise what a hostile environment motorsport would be for them, not because of the nature of the work or because it's a difficult route to success, but because of the implicit biases that still exist purely because of their gender.

Thankfully, in a similar way that I and many other Black and ethnic minority members of the paddock have been working towards breaking down these barriers, there are some incredibly talented women trying to change the landscape. While for many years, marketing and hospitality roles have been commonly dominated by women (although this does tend to change as you look up towards the top of the management structure), people like Hannah Schmitz, Ruth Buscombe and Bernie Collins have spent years on the frontline of the battle for women in technical roles. Their work isn't for nothing, as we're finally seeing more women wanting to take on careers in these disciplines and, thanks to their willingness to speak about their time in the sport, I believe that many more will follow in their footsteps.

It's up to all of us to make the environment more inclusive and call out behaviours that are unacceptable. For all of those working in the sport now, don't think for one second that simply not being responsible for this behaviour yourselves is enough. I will always take the view that if you know of or witness these injustices and you choose not to speak out about them at all, then you are complicit in allowing them to continue. While I accept that you may not be in a position to do much about it (as I've found myself plenty of times over the years), there will be someone in your organisation that you can report it to, and that's a start. On quite a few occasions I've found myself in positions where speaking out isn't easy, but it is necessary, even if that means just confronting that person in private. If you witness some shitty behaviour and don't even address it with the person responsible, you've let them know that they can continue, essentially, with your blessing.

Selfishly, it took me far too long to recognise some of the biases that women in the sport face – the ones that I myself was in the privileged position of not having to worry about. Now I have a daughter, I'm forced to consider whether I would want her to have to work in what can be an incredibly intimidating environment for young women in the paddock. Once I realised that the answer was 'No, of course I wouldn't', I knew that, to avoid being part of the problem, I would need to be part of the solution. I'd like to think that all of the women that I work with now know that I wouldn't hesitate to speak up if I found out that they were being mistreated.

When I was asked to provide that case study about my career as part of the research for the Hamilton Commission report, I viewed it as a way to help others. What I didn't realise was that it would be just as helpful to me.

One of the ways that getting involved helped me was by connecting me with a community of Black and ethnic minority engineers, mechanics and designers, as well as people doing a whole host of other jobs in the motorsport sector. I'd become so used to working with so few people of colour early on in my career that I had to embrace it as a challenge. I didn't look to anyone for representation, because there was nobody to look to. Had these communities existed when I was younger, I'm certain that I would have discovered racing as a potential career far sooner. Being connected to the some of the many Black and ethnic minority engineers trying to forge careers in racing was inspiring for me, and I rediscovered how powerful it was to have a community behind you.

Many of the people I first met through a shared interest in creating a more inclusive and diverse sport are now members of the UK motorsport club Driven By Us. Founded in 2021 by James Dornor, a former F1 systems engineer at Mercedes, Driven By Us work to empower underrepresented groups in motorsport. With a network of people to give advice and expertise, as well as offering careers events and highlighting opportunities within the sector, their work is already making a difference. If you think that you could be a future race engineer in the making or are just interested in careers in the industry, I strongly suggest that you look at some of the work that Driven by Us are doing.

When I talk about diversity and inclusion in motorsport, I often feel like I'm having to sell the idea to people. 'We don't like change' has been a common stance for teams to take on many things and, for many years, diversity was one of those. When Sir Lewis Hamilton started raising the issues, a lot of people of colour already working in the industry found themselves having to 'sell' diversity and inclusion, not because the organisations that they worked for were inherently racist, but just because people tend to reject change if there isn't a reason that they can easily understand.

When talking about the need for diversity in any business or team, I tend to say that there are two reasons why it's beneficial. The first is what I'd call the humanitarian reason. Most intelligent, well-rounded people tend to agree that having a level playing field in life and allowing everyone to have an equal opportunity to succeed is just the right thing to do. It really is as simple as that. Even since the launch of the Hamilton Commission, coupled with work undertaken by the organisations trying to break down barriers to access, some in the sport still just don't get that.

The second benefit is that it can have a positive result in terms of business. We live in a world where capitalism rules and, because of that, 'the right thing to do' may not seem particularly appealing to many profit-seeking enterprises. A lot of businesses just don't see where there is a return on investment into things like diversity and inclusion strategies. However, having a diverse workforce has productivity and performance benefits for any business. Everybody looks to solve problems in their own ways. The way that you look at problems will be a direct reflection of the environment in which you learned these skills. People from different cultures, ethnicities, genders and socio-economic backgrounds will all view problems differently and find different ways to overcome them. As such, having a diverse workforce is far more likely to provide diversity of thought and generate many more solutions to a given problem. This has been proven by plenty of studies, which show diverse workforces are far more productive and perform better.

In racing, that will translate directly to performance. Engineering is basically just problem solving. We want a particular outcome; how do we get there? A team of designers with a wider range of ideas on how to solve that problem are far more likely to produce the best solution than a group of people who have all lived similar experiences and received the same education from the same institutions. In racing, that higher productivity can therefore directly relate to on-track performance. So, when a business asks, 'What's in it for us?', that's the answer.

When it comes to how we make change in the industry, there are always going to be different views about the best way to achieve a more inclusive environment in motorsport. My view will always be that long-term solutions that tackle the root causes of a lack of diversity in the industry are the ones that we would be best served by pursuing. I hate window dressing. As a concept, affirmative action – the policy of hiring people based on characteristics such as ethnicity or gender, in order to fill 'quotas' – is just as offensive to me as not hiring someone because of these characteristics. There are multiple issues raised when these kinds of programmes take a foothold in any industry. For one, and the most important in my view, is that it is not a lasting solution. As an example, if I were to hire six underqualified or unsuitable Black mechanics to take on roles in a race team, while it would do a great job of providing visual representation for a short time (nobody does this job for ever), that initiative would do absolutely nothing to break down the barriers that resulted in that group of people being underrepresented in the first place. It would also do nothing to educate and inspire the next generation of potential engineering talent, meaning that when those mechanics that I hired inevitably retire, we'd likely be worse off than when we started. Masking the fundamental issues would mean that, in this situation, not only would we still be lacking a diverse talent pool in the industry, but we would have also failed to tackle any of the actual barriers, while pretending that they didn't exist.

This is something I've become acutely aware of as my own profile has been growing. As a result, I've been making every effort to speak about and work towards breaking down these barriers to access. I didn't want people to use my success or prominence as 'proof' that these barriers didn't exist. They do, and they're wide ranging.

Affirmative action also poses a number of issues for Black and ethnic minority people already working in the sport. An issue with these kinds of programmes is that as soon as they become public knowledge, the efforts of those who have worked tirelessly to build themselves careers in the industry are immediately diminished. Critics will now have the perfect weapon to dismiss their achievements. If these hiring practices were to take a foothold in the sport, and Black people who succeed in the future were then subjected to these 'diversity hire' accusations as well as dealing with many other barriers, then arguably we will have made the environment even more hostile than it was when I started in 2009.

In my own case, being branded a 'token' or 'diversity hire' by those looking to disparage me began almost as soon as Red Bull Racing started regularly winning again. Many people online tried to paint me as some sort of 'race traitor'. Like I was somehow less Black for not choosing to work at Mercedes and supporting Lewis. I've never really understood how somebody would come to that conclusion based on who my employer is. On more than one occasion, people have sent me messages asking how I could possibly work for Red Bull Racing, calling us a 'racist' team and accusing me of being a traitor for competing against the only Black driver in the sport.

I never want to give these people the satisfaction of a reply, but I will say this about my experience at the team over the last decade. The place isn't perfect and neither am I – it can be a tense and stressful environment, and I've had plenty of heated exchanges and fallings out with my colleagues over the years. But I can categorically say that's it's never been about my ethnicity. Ability (and the occasional bit of politics) is the only thing that matters to people who just want to win. Red Bull Racing can be a ruthless place in that sense, for sure, but it's not systemically racist. That really isn't the nature of the people I've worked alongside for the last decade. While I accept that the team hasn't done itself many favours over the years in terms of its public image relating to these things, it's a much more inclusive space than social media will have you believe. That's been my experience anyway. Being the most visible person of colour in the team, the one that's on people's TV screens each week, and having a growing social media presence, I'm often expected by some to publicly share my opinions on controversies that senior management have caused. Helmut Marko's comments about Sergio Pérez just prior to the 2023 Singapore Grand Prix put me in a really tight spot in that sense. The messages and abuse I receive whenever something like this occurs always feel grossly unfair. The reality for me in these situations is that taking to social media to express my dissatisfaction isn't going to make the situation any better. Instead, I voice my concerns within the team – that's what I'm supposed to do! I'm far more interested in resolving the issues than telling the world that I too disagree with the comments made. In an ideal world – where I didn't have to worry about throwing away a career that I've spent half my life building – perhaps I might have been more inclined to be publicly vocal about it all but, in reality, it wouldn't have changed anything. As I've said previously, in situations like this one, I do find myself powerless and I just have to accept there are still some attitudes in the sport that need to play themselves out. So, while on plenty of occasions I might have been tempted, I just knew that it wouldn't be beneficial and it wouldn't have done anything to break down the actual barriers to the sport that people from different ethnicities face. To suggest that everyone in the team who doesn't publicly speak out against their bosses is complicit simply isn't a fair reflection of the situations we find ourselves in.

In some ways, these accusations of being a 'coconut' are almost amusing, because they're so far detached from the reality – in particular, the classic 'diversity hire' claims. Having joined the paddock at a time when the sport had absolutely no interest in even recognising that there were access issues for Black and ethnic minority people, let alone making any sort of effort to rectify them, I found the 'token' label to be pretty absurd. It's even funnier when you consider that over the years there have been plenty of people in the sport who, unhappy about my growing profile, sought to stop my voice being amplified. Again, this wasn't because of my ethnicity either: they just didn't want someone at my level having a growing public profile.

While I've found these accusations often come from disgruntled people whose issue tends to be my team affiliation rather than a genuine concern about hiring practices in the sport, they should still be considered very offensive. Even with the security and confidence of someone who's spent over a decade in the pitlane, I can understand how emotionally damaging the 'token' accusation can be.

While I firmly believe that the sport should always remain a meritocracy, I also know that a meritocracy only has true value if the same opportunity is available to all. This is why, rather than simply encouraging teams to change their hiring practices, I tend to focus my energy on promoting careers to those who may not pursue them otherwise and encouraging those with the power to do so to break down the barriers that prevent people from pursuing these careers in the first place. If awareness of opportunity and highlighting the vast number of different possibilities available to people are something that I can contribute towards, then that's what I have a responsibility to do. I could never be the type of person to succeed against the odds and then pull the ladder up behind me.

If Formula One and its teams really want to effect long-term change, then I think the focus and investment need to be in education. What I'd really like to see is Formula One Management and the teams partnering with multiple junior formula teams to provide funded apprenticeships to deserving students from a wide range of socio-economic backgrounds. Creating a pathway that allows more mechanics to fight for a place in the F1 paddock, and earning while they train, would be an incredibly effective tool.

One of the barriers that I faced, when I decided to pursue a career in racing, was financial. I didn't receive any government funding when I went back to college, but I was unable to work much while I was there three days a week, and meanwhile I had to pay for travel and lodgings to train outside of the city I lived in. Going back to college was only possible because my parents could afford to support me for that period. Without that support, I wouldn't have a career in racing – it's as simple as that. I was incredibly lucky. The truth is that in the UK, for a large proportion of Black and ethnic minority families, funding a twenty-year-old in this manner simply isn't possible. There's so much untapped talent in young people in our inner cities that, for financial reasons, will never get put on display. Paid apprenticeships could really help to level the playing field. With F1 being more profitable than ever, we could make a huge difference!

When looking at how people go from education to employment, hiring practices are changing. Many teams are trying to make their application processes fairer and trying to remove the opportunity for implicit biases to be a factor in selecting successful candidates. Practices such as sending hiring managers 'blind' CV's, with no names or faces on, are being used by teams to great effect. In an ideal world, of course, people who hold discriminatory views wouldn't find themselves in those hiring positions, but it's not an ideal world. I believe that we will get closer to that point, we're just not there yet. We're talking about an industry that really only started to consider changing its thinking five years ago. The old boys' club hasn't been disbanded and it's still very powerful within the sport. The old boys won't last, though. As each generation makes its way through the industry and the old guard retires, things will only get better.

I had this discussion with an HR rep back in 2023 and we agreed that, fortunately, while 'teaching old dogs new tricks' in upper management is never likely to succeed, those people won't be around for ever. What we can do is ensure that those who will replace them are ready to lead in a more inclusive way. We can do that by putting in the work to train and prepare these personnel now.

When I do eventually step down from life in the Formula One pitlane, it may currently seem that a large portion of representation for Black engineers within the sport will go with me. Thankfully, there are now many other talented Black technicians throughout the Formula One paddock and I'm certain that the number will grow, but they'll need the support of their teams to amplify their voices, and this isn't something that is guaranteed.

It's for this reason that I've spent the last few years working on projects that aim to find long-term solutions. In particular, I try to give my time to projects that focus on awareness and education in STEM, and, most importantly, help young people about to make important decisions about their lives as they choose what they will study at GCSE level. I also try to encourage large organisations like Red Bull Racing to do the same. I'm very grateful for Red Bull for always allowing me the freedom to speak about these things and build a profile of my own. They didn't have to, but they saw the value in allowing me to reach an audience that really wasn't being reached through the usual outlets.

As a result of my interest in diversity and inclusion in motorsport, one organisation that I was fortunate to discover (through the network that Driven By Us has built) was the Blair Project. Founded by Nile Henry along with his racing-driver brother Blair, the non-profit organisation aims to engage young people in STEM while promoting sustainable motorsport. Finding time in 2023 to get involved in their ProtoEV challenge, I was absolutely amazed to see how well such a small organisation could engage young people in motorsport through a hands-on learning experience. The ProtoEV challenge works with youth centres from some of the most deprived areas in the UK. Providing each of these youth groups with an old petrol-powered go-kart, the challenge requires each group to understand, strip down and then rebuild the kart as an electric vehicle. The charity provides all of the parts and resources needed to complete the build.

After attending one of their testing days at a very cold and windy karting track in south London, I left with a real desire to do more. Some of the knowledge that these kids had already gained during the process was impressive, and their reaction to my attendance really did make me quite emotional. Just being able to help give these young people the confidence to continue learning and improving felt like a real privilege. I made the long drive back to Northampton thinking about how I could find some more time for this kind of work during such a demanding Formula One season. It's initiatives like these that, with the support of the teams, Formula One Management and the governing bodies, will likely have the most positive long-term impact on changing the demographic of people who want to have the skillset required to work in the sport.

I was so pleased to hear, from one of Red Bull Racing's cultural group representatives in 2024, that the team were in discussions with the Blair Project as to how they might be able to assist going forward. Even if that's only giving its employees the opportunity to volunteer their time, this alone raises awareness, which is one of the Blair Project's goals.

Ultimately, initiatives like this need two big things: funding and exposure. These are things that all organisations within Formula One can help with, if they want to.

CHAPTER 10

The Cost of the Cost Cap

The new set of FIA financial regulations introduced at the start of the 2021 season, applying to all teams competing in Formula One, aimed to level the playing field and close the gap in performance between the teams at either end of the grid. It was the intention of Formula One Management to make the sport more financially sustainable, with the apparent goal of enticing more large manufacturers into the sport and keeping those who'd struggled with rising costs. The idea was that by restricting how much the bigger outfits could spend on the research and development of their cars, the smaller teams would stand a better chance of competing and fighting for wins over the course of the season.

As an additional measure, teams were restricted in how many hours of wind-tunnel time they could use, which was allocated differently according to where teams stood in the championship at different periods. Long ago, wind-tunnel time was unrestricted, meaning that the teams with the most money could run their wind tunnels almost twenty-four/seven. More recently, teams' aerodynamic testing has been restricted. The allowed wind-tunnel and CFD (Computational Fluid Dynamics) time for each team is now allocated on a sliding scale, based on constructors' championship standings from the previous period.

In 2021, this meant that the team that won the previous year's constructors' championship, Mercedes, were allotted only 90 per cent of the average testing allocation, equating to thirty-six runs per week. Williams, at the other end of the previous year's standings, were allotted 112.5 per cent, or forty-five runs per week. This sliding scale became even more severe for the 2022 season and has remained in place since. It's an effective system for removing some of the financial imbalance between teams and how it affects their ability to carry out aerodynamic testing and bring upgrades to the car. Prior to these rules, the top teams were bringing aero upgrades to the cars every single week, making the task of closing the gap almost impossible for the chasing pack.

The cost cap has been a contentious issue since its introduction, with Red Bull and Aston Martin both falling foul of the FIA's expectations upon review of the first season's spending. Overall, my view is that some form of financial regulation throughout the sport was necessary. Certainly, since COVID and the resulting increase in inflation in Europe, the costs to run a Formula One team had grown astronomically. The air- and sea-freight costs alone had increased at a seemingly exponential rate. It would be fair to say that without the introduction of the FIA's financial regulations, three or four teams would no longer be in the sport, or at least in their current guise. The financial struggles of both Williams and McLaren were well documented in the few years prior to 2021 and without being able to attract the incoming investment from Audi, you'd have to wonder how long Sauber could have continued as an independent customer team.

During my time at Marussia, while we knew we were unlikely to ever compete at the sharp end of the championship, the difference between beating Caterham and finishing tenth in the constructors' championship and finishing eleventh was huge financially. 'Drive to survive', rather than just a pithy title for a Netflix series, used to be a reality for us every single week. When the team collapsed along with Caterham in 2014, it wasn't a great look for motorsport that the running costs had become so high that teams competing at its pinnacle couldn't sustain themselves financially. This apparent lack of profitability was also something that would likely dissuade new manufacturers from considering entering the sport. Formula One Management had to find a solution.

*

I'm not against trying to level the playing field for the sake of creating better racing and closer championships. While I consider myself a racing purist, and I certainly don't want to hold back development in what we often consider to be the peak of motorsport engineering, I do also accept that providing entertainment is a requirement for the sport's survival and growth. As a concept, regulating how teams spend money and how much they can spend seemed like a good way to curb the insane amounts that were spent prior to the introduction of the cap. Back in 2017, Ferrari, Mercedes and Red Bull were spending between £250 and £300 million a year to go racing. When competing at the front of the grid, recouping much of this was far easier as the outfits performing well would naturally be more attractive to sponsors. However, for those teams at the lower end of the order, attracting enough sponsorship to have the income needed to push their way up was a difficult task. Teams found that once that gap between themselves and the front runners had been created, it was an almost impossible task to close it – they were always a step behind. The cap aimed to break that cycle.

Although I'm not averse to financial regulation in Formula One, in its current guise, I think it's a slowly approaching disaster. I think that Formula One's management and the FIA need to reconsider many of the ways in which the cost cap is applied, and redefine how some activities are viewed in terms of their benefit to a team's performance. Just as importantly, now that the cap has been in place for some time, I feel that we need to try and better define the inclusions to the cap and simplify the regulations. If you've ever been unfortunate enough to have tried to read through and understand all the financial regulations, you'll understand what I mean. It's a minefield of legal jargon.

At some point in 2021, I asked Jonathan Wheatley a question relating to filling out my timesheets (a requirement for everyone since the introduction of the cap). Jonathan simply replied by sending me a link to the regulations document on the FIA website and left me to work it out. After about twenty minutes of trying to understand the section relating to my question, I had a headache. I remembered this a year later, when it was announced that Aston Martin and Red Bull had been found to be in breach of the 2021 cap, with the former found to have fallen foul in some kind of procedural manner.

The rules are ridiculously complicated. This is partly due to the different structures of the different businesses operating in the sport and the need to make sure all situations are covered. You can't force large corporations to restructure an entire business in order to make them all the same, it wouldn't work, but the FIA still needed to ensure that the larger teams couldn't use their advanced company structures to skirt the rules. As such, each amendment aimed at closing any potential loophole just seemed to be piled on top of the last, resulting in an assault course of convoluted wording for which teams ended up employing entire accounting departments to navigate.

Early on, when the regulations were put in place, teams were constantly back and forth with the FIA, questioning what could be considered an 'in-cap' cost any time that the wording of the rules could allow for different interpretations. As with anything else in the sport, this process in itself became quite political. One philosophy was that when you think something could be excluded from the cap, but you would want it included, you would ask the question to the FIA, in the hope that they would issue a clarification to all teams that a particular spend would be considered 'in-cap'. The other would be to interpret something written in the regulations in the way that suited you, considering a cost 'out of cap' and then pleading plausible deniability if it later transpired that the FIA considered it an 'in-cap' cost. This kind of thing was rife in the first year of the new regulations, as could be expected.

My biggest gripe with the cap in its current form, however, isn't with the complicated rules. It is related to what is and isn't included, and how each inclusion relates to a team's ability to develop a race car and improve on-track performance. With the rules as they are currently, their impact has been more far-reaching than simply an attempt to level the playing field among teams.

Currently, those who are suffering, and who will continue to suffer the most long term, are the lowest earners working in the sport. The decision to include all salaries as an in-cap cost, excluding only drivers, a team's top three earners and those working in marketing and communications, is a huge blow to all the designers, engineers, mechanics and technicians that make Formula One work. It almost feels cynical – a rule that now gives multi-million-pound businesses the perfect excuse to pay highly skilled workers less than they are worth. All of this during an almost unprecedented cost-of-living crisis in the West, yet we're now in an era where all Formula One teams are profitable businesses. Gone are the days where teams could take on losses year on year, struggling to stay afloat. Business is booming for Formula One teams . . . but not for the individuals working behind the scenes in F1.

The problem with salaries being included, in the way that they are currently, is that it forces every team to choose between paying their staff and developing their car. In an industry where winning is everything, there's only ever going to be one winner in that trade-off. Wage stagnation is going to become an issue for all teams if the current rules continue as they are. I'd argue that those whose roles involve travelling to all events have been worst affected. As the calendar continues to grow, those who travel are physically required to do more work, spend more time away from their families and miss out on more of their lives, for no more pay.

The long-term problem that this presents is simply that the best minds, and the best people for these jobs, are reaching the point where they can earn more by taking their talents to other industries. I already know of line managers throughout the sport who, when hiring for roles in teams, are considering the cheapest person for the job, rather than the best person for the job. This is a dangerous race to the bottom, and one that's very hard to come back from. If it continues and leads to a 'brain drain' in the industry, for how long can Formula One consider itself the pinnacle of motorsport engineering?

Some teams have come up with novel ideas to skirt these rules on salaries (and I applaud them for doing so). Using bonuses, which are outside of the cap, a few teams have tried to fairly compensate staff as their workload increases. At Alpine, travelling technicians receive a bonus of £1,000 for every race that they attend beyond sixteen. At Mercedes, salaries and bonuses were restructured to a fair degree in order to keep as many of these costs as possible out of the cap. I'm sure such schemes exist among most teams in the paddock.

Red Bull's ability to retain staff over the years has been largely down to the working environment and the winning culture of the team, as opposed to being the highest payers. Red Bull have never been the highest paying team in the paddock, as far as I'm aware – that's been an accolade awarded to McLaren for a long time, partly due to their factory being located in one of the more expensive areas in England to live. Over the last few years, at least since 2022, Red Bull Racing have been essentially getting away with stagnating wages because they've been winning.

After a record-breaking 2023 season, individuals in the team raked in around £15,000 in bonuses for the calendar year. This is all well and good while it lasts but, as we all know, no team keeps winning for ever. Bonuses are not guaranteed income and the general fear is that once the race-win and championship bonuses start to dwindle as the field becomes more competitive, staff retention could become more difficult.

A fair number of people have already chosen to move over to Red Bull Advanced Technologies, working on the RB17 and other projects outside of the Formula One cap. It's perfectly understandable. While many of these people clearly do still love racing and want to stay within the Red Bull family, at some point a financial decision has to be made if an opportunity arises to bring your salary out of the cap.

I don't like to be the voice of problems without offering solutions, and I think there is a suitable solution for this particular negative effect of the financial regulations. In my view, rather than including salaries in the total allowable spend of teams, the FIA should instead define the number of people a team can employ for F1 activities. This is something that's already been in force for trackside personnel for some time. For many years now, teams have only been allowed to have 'sixty operational personnel' at the circuit, that's sixty people whose jobs are directly related to running the cars, in the paddock, at any one time. It works. Without this rule and the operational curfews in place, the top teams would use their greater numbers to send more people to the circuit and essentially put on shifts, day and night, throughout the week. The operational personnel limit levelled the playing field in that regard.

I struggle to see why a similar approach couldn't work to remove the salary issue. I would suggest that if it were applied company-wide as a replacement for having in-cap salary costs, these personnel limits could be further defined by department. Defining clearly how many heads teams could have in each area of the company, working on F1-related projects, would seem a much fairer way to bring equality to the paddock. This method would mean a return to allowing highly skilled personnel to earn what they are worth, and promote the meritocracy in the competitive job market that is Formula One, rather than forcing the larger outfits to constantly trade employee welfare for car performance.

I discussed this topic with Sky Sports' David Croft (aka Crofty) during the weekend of Bahrain 2024. We agreed that something will have to give in this battle. He felt that perhaps another solution would be to review the cap year-on-year, and balance inflation and the cost of living in the countries where each team were based with an additional spending allowance. This would be a unique amount for each team, and would only be useable by teams if spent on staff wages. While I agreed that this too could work, I worry that it might just create even more loopholes and obstacles in the wording of the regulations that teams would have to navigate. As a way of simplification, I felt my suggestion might work better for everyone.

There are other ways in which the definition of what is in-cap and what is out creates issues that teams have to navigate in a manner that's not conducive to efficient working practices. One of these problems relates to Formula One's 'net zero' targets. While we're all supposed to be working towards a more sustainable and environmentally responsible sport, there are financial regulations in place that force teams to operate in a manner that defies these goals entirely.

As an example, the salaries of marketing and communications personnel, as I mentioned earlier, are currently not an in-cap cost. In order to ensure that teams don't try to exploit this rule, a section of the financial regulations makes clear that F1 activities and marketing activities cannot be conflated (to try and disguise an in-cap cost as a marketing activity). There needed to be clear separation in terms of spending. This immediately led to a new problem. Teams often travel by coach to and from airports, as one would expect. One would also expect that provided a coach has the capacity, and all personnel are travelling to and from the same place, everyone on a particular trip would use one coach. This was how it had been for most of my time in F1. However, the new financial regulations that stated that any marketing costs had to be completely separate from F1 activity costs meant that the marketing personnel could no longer share a coach with the race team.

If a member of the marketing team were to hop on the coach with the race team to the airport, there's a fair risk that, if discovered, it would pull that person's entire salary into the cost cap. Simultaneously, if a member of the race team were to hop on the marketing coach, it could pull the cost of that entire coach into the cap. It's ridiculous, as well as environmentally unfriendly and more expensive, to put on an extra coach while leaving plenty of empty seats on the first one, but this is currently the reality.

Further to this, when the F1 calendar used to take us from Spa-Francorchamps in Belgium to Zandvoort in the neighbouring Netherlands, the team used to fly from one to the other, all of twenty minutes, rather than take the quite enjoyable drive for a few hours in the rental vehicles. Of course, overall, it was much quicker to hop in vans and drive, as we did in the first year of the Dutch Grand Prix's return to the calendar in 2021, but the financial regulations incentivised the team to change that the following year. This is because, while rental vehicles and track transfers were an in-cap cost, flights were not.

So, despite it being far less economical and financially frugal overall, it was more beneficial to spend the extra money and fly so that we could lower the amount of money spent on the rental vehicles, thereby freeing up space in the cap – all the while providing an unwanted contribution to climate change in direct defiance of the sport's 'net zero' goals. It's quite frankly absurd.

I think that I understand exactly how we got to this point with the rules around travel. Picture the meetings between team bosses and the sport's management when deciding these rules. As the working groups that help to form the regulations go through different aspects and costs, and decide what should and shouldn't be included, at some point they get to the issue of travel.

'What about flights?' says somebody important at one end of the table.

All of the CEOs look at one another, knowing full well that if air travel becomes something that is included as an in-cap cost, it would be the end of their first-class seats and private jets. As a result, it shouldn't really be surprising that flights were excluded.

What other explanation can I offer to explain why flying would not be included in the spending limitations, but driving to and from the circuit in a rental vehicle would be? It's not as though, by excluding the cost of flying, the expense has gone away. Travel for personnel is still one of the most expensive parts of running a race team. So excluding flying from the cap serves only to protect the few whose travel costs are significantly more than those of everyone else. In the same way that excluding the drivers and top three earners' salaries does, the financial rules around travel as they're currently structured simply protect those at the top.

*

The cost-cap regulations are now so far reaching that I've also seen first-hand just how difficult it can be to navigate them, even when trying to engage in activities not remotely related to racing. Through my work with Red Bull Racing's 'Inclusioneers', the employee resource groups working to make the team more inclusive, I've seen the extra strain that has been placed on human resources when trying to put on events aimed at inspiring young engineers and attracting people into the sport.

As an example, I often volunteer to speak at some of the brilliant events that are held in the amazing facility we have in MK7. Whenever I do, I'm reminded that Red Bull employees are not permitted to consume any of the food laid on for guests of the event. Technically, as a member of the race team, if I were to grab a sandwich, or perhaps a handful of crisps, while talking to a group of graduate engineers, I'd run the risk of dragging the entire cost of catering for that event into the cap. An expensive sandwich.

All of these hoops that teams now have to jump through in order to do things that we ideally want to encourage, mean that unfortunately, from a diversity and inclusion perspective, we'll likely make slower progress than we should. At Red Bull Racing, the in-cap budget is closely guarded by our technical director, Pierre Waché. As much as I love Pierre, I wouldn't have wanted to be one of the HR leads, who in the early days of the regulations, were having to ask his permission to spend a couple of thousand pounds that might end up coming out of the cap depending on how an event was interpreted. It's the red tape in areas like this that desperately needs removing.

I suppose it wouldn't be right for me to discuss the financial regulations, or catering costs, without addressing how Red Bull fell foul of the rules in the 2021 season. A lot of jokes on social media are still made about 'catering' costs at Red Bull. When people used to tag me in social media posts relating to catering, it usually made me chuckle – mostly because I've never been the biggest fan of the food anyway, but also because, in typical fashion, whenever there's anything perceived as negative about the team in the news, there is always a group that behave as though I'm somehow personally responsible. The Twitterati always seem to expect me to have the answers to every going-on within the team or larger business. It's like they forget that I'm just one of a group of lowly mechanics and technicians. I have a social media profile, but I'm entirely clueless about the business's accounting practices. I'm also not an official spokesperson for the team. I just assemble engines.

Beyond what was reported by the media and the odd bit of paddock gossip, I really don't know the full ins and outs of what led to the team's breach of the regulations and subsequent punishment. From my understanding, the infringement was related to a Red Bull policy, throughout all of its entities, to provide free and subsidised meals to their staff.

The food available on the campus in MK7 has always been heavily subsidised since I started in 2015 but, a little while before the financial regulations were introduced, the team started providing entirely free meals to all staff. Using an app that would generate a QR code, all Red Bull Racing employees get a minimum of £5 per day to spend on food. If your shift is longer than eight hours or over a weekend, that free-spend amount goes up. This might not sound a lot and certainly, if you were working in Westminster, £5 wouldn't get you a lot for lunch, but as the food in MK7 is still heavily subsidised, that money can go a long way.

For the few days a year I'd spend in the factory over the course of the season, I'd always go and treat myself to a full English breakfast prior to pitstop practice. Two eggs, sausages, bacon, beans, hash browns and a couple of slices of toast later, and the total would come to around £4. It was ridiculously cheap (and I think quite impressive that I'd manage to do pitstops after eating that much). I'd challenge anyone to find a decent fry-up in the UK for under a fiver.

When it was first reported that this subsidised food scheme was at the heart of a breach of the financial regulations, it pissed me off, to be perfectly honest. It meant that this was viewed as a 'benefit in kind' for all staff and therefore liable to be considered an in-cap cost. I wasn't pissed off because the rules had been enforced, or that I felt we should have been allowed any sort of exemption. I was pissed off because even if we agree that these meals are indeed a benefit in kind, I fail to see how that in any way poses an unfair advantage in terms of a team's performance. Yes, you could argue that it makes the company more attractive to work for compared to others who don't provide this, but it's beyond a stretch to suggest it would improve the performance of the team. Furthermore, with salaries as an in-cap cost, there's only so many people that the team can employ and pay anyway.

Mostly I was annoyed because free meals are a great thing that a company can do for its employees, and it should be applauded. It baffled me that rather than encourage the other multi-million-pound race teams to do more for their lowest paid staff during a cost-of-living crisis, many in the sport chose to try and shame Red Bull over what I would consider a fairly minor infringement.

I firmly believe that any breach of the rules has to be punished in accordance with those rules and Red Bull Racing rightly were, but I feel that the incident was a perfect example of a missed opportunity to review what we consider to be beneficial for the health of the sport, its future, and the people who work in it, under these new regulations. Punishment aside, I would have liked to have seen more voices in the sport ask why we weren't encouraging teams to do more for their staff, and demand that we need some reform of these punitive parts of the rules that offer fans nothing towards the quality of the racing.

In summary, I'd like to see the FIA's financial regulations reworked. Firstly, I'd like to see the welfare of those working at all levels in the sport considered a priority when creating rules around salaries. Secondly, I'd like to see an overall simplification of the regulations, with only things directly related to the design, development, manufacturing and logistical costs of running a Formula One car included in the spend cap. Staff wages need to be excluded from the spending cap. As long as they remain an in-cap cost, the sport's governing body is giving multi-million-pound companies the perfect excuse to pay talented people less than they are worth, and that is a terrible precedent to set.

I think that both of these changes will happen in time, but for those working in the sport, they really can't come soon enough.

CHAPTER 11

All or Nothing

Fifteen years of racing, two Le Mans, thirteen Formula One seasons, two hundred and thirty-three Grands Prix, four World Drivers' Championships, two World Constructors' Championships, seven consecutive pitstop awards . . . it's a career that I'm incredibly proud to look back on.

I've achieved more than I could have ever dreamed. I've been around the world ten times, seen the sights, experienced the cultures and enjoyed the sweet taste of victory. As I sit here writing this, thinking of that two-second pitstop adrenaline rush that I still live for, I wonder how well (or poorly) I might adjust to life after the pitlane. Even if I go on to spend time in the paddock doing other stuff, nothing will compare to the thrill of being in the pitlane mid-race as a car comes speeding towards you for a pitstop.

When I do decide to call it a day, I'll even miss some of the hardest parts of the job: the unsociable hours, the travel, even the physical strain. For every bad day at the track, I can tell you about ten great ones, so on balance, I can't think of anything that I would rather have done for a living for this huge period of my life.

It's a great privilege to find a career that you truly love and can earn a living from. It's even greater when it's enabled you to travel the world doing something so extraordinary. The thing that amazes me most, when I look back on my time as a race technician, is that even after all of the travel and all of the successes, year after year, I never get bored of it. That buzz on a Sunday morning won't ever go away.

The other great thing about any engineering career is that I'll never stop learning. 'Every day is a school day' is a phrase that I think applies to racing more than any other industry that I've experienced. People often think that, after all this time, I must be somewhat immune to the amazing technology or the skill of the drivers. That couldn't be further from the truth. While it may not always show on my face during the Saturday afternoon of the third weekend in a triple-header, I'd still rather be working at a racetrack as opposed to having been sitting in an office for the last fifteen years.

If you plan on pursuing a career travelling as a Formula One race mechanic, in order to succeed, you'll have to make some sacrifices on the way. Your time with friends, family and even for yourself is at the behest of a twenty-four-race calendar spanning from February through to December. Fraught with double- and triple-headers, pre- and post-season testing and long shifts building the new car each January, there really is very little rest for those who choose it as a career.

With that said, it's the best job I've ever had and, given everything I know now, I'd most likely do it all again. Short of joining the military, there really aren't many jobs that will take you around the globe, working with your hands for two hundred days of the year, and while motorsport can be dangerous (it says so on the ticket), I can gladly say that I have never been shot at while at work.

It's great that the job isn't easy. If it was, anyone could do it. To a certain extent, I think that it should be difficult to succeed at the very pinnacle of a sport. That's why you'll be proud of the successes when you achieve them. It takes a particularly nomadic personality to choose to spend nearly two hundred days a year away from home. The work is rarely glamorous, the hours are long and it can be both stressful and heartbreaking, but when you win, you'll soon understand why it's all worth it!

I'm aware that, at this current juncture in my life, the sacrifices being made so that I can continue doing what I love are no longer just my own. My partner, Phoebe, the woman I met in the F1 paddock over a decade ago and fell in love with, has made some of the biggest sacrifices you could ever ask of someone in support of your dreams. With our daughter, Isabella, I feel like each time I pack a case and head to the airport, the sacrifice that she makes grows larger. So many of my colleagues with young children will tell you just how hard it is to leave when your child is asking you not to go, but you have to. It's heartbreaking. Now, when I come home from a triple-header, I feel like I've missed huge chunks of her life. I think I'm reaching a point, having surpassed every target I set for myself back in 2009, where I need to consider making some sacrifices for them.

It's not an easy thing to do – to move on from something you truly love doing. While there are opportunities for me to take a different career path while remaining in the sport that I love, it's taken me a while to come to terms with just how much I will miss being in that garage, in the thick of it, when I do decide to move on.

I didn't spend this long in the pitlane for the money – no Formula One mechanic does. There are plenty of mechanics in the F1 paddock who have been there far longer than me and they'll all tell you the same thing: the truth is that a good technician can make more money for way less effort than they will in F1. I spent this long here because I love the cars, I love the technology and I love the competition. I love the smell of a raging hot race car coming in for a pitstop. I love a tight qualifying session. I love the noise just before the lights go out on a Sunday afternoon. I love the struggle, the effort and the teamwork that goes into winning. I love those lucky moments that seem to arrive just when you need them most. I love the tough days and the glorious ones. I love racing. That love of racing is something that you'll need too, if you plan on having a long and fruitful career in the paddock. There's no half-arsing it – you're in or you're out. It's all or nothing. I've seen plenty of mechanics come and go in no time at all, not because they weren't skilled enough, but because they were never cut out for the lifestyle in the first place: they didn't love it enough.

People talk about legacy in sport, and often I'm asked what I want my legacy to be when I decide to hang up my race suit. I guess, for me, the most important thing would be that I'm able to say that I inspired people. The sport moves so fast that very few leave a lasting impression on its history. In the same way that, in my mind, Lewis Hamilton's greatest achievements will be what he's doing off the track – what he's doing for the next generation of talent in the industry – I'd just like to be able to say that I used my career to inspire someone. This especially applies to those who saw an industry that for so long seemed to be an exclusive club, and thought that they would never be able to be part of it.

I hope that I'm on the right path to teaching my daughter that she can achieve anything if she's willing to do what it takes to turn her goals into achievements. If this book, along with what I've achieved through perseverance, inspires her, then that's probably the best legacy I could ask for.

I also hope people like my friend fifteen years ago, who said that 'they ain't gonna let you in' because I'm a Black man, now know that, even if that sort of thing is true in any given moment, you can be the one to change it!

I can say that the sport has grown, has evolved and has changed for the better. We still have a way to go, we still have barriers to accessing the sport that we need to tear down, but if my legacy is that I provided the representation for people of colour that I never had when I started, then I'll be happy.

Acknowledgements

Turning this book from an idea into reality was an incredible journey and I'd like to thank the special people who have made it possible:

My manager Francesca Scambler, and everyone at District Global, as well as my literary agent Oscar Janson-Smith, thanks for your passion and drive to get this project done, and for your patience with me and my schedule. Thank you to Zoe Bohm and all the team at Piatkus for having faith in me to create something of value, and for steering me in the right direction. It's been an incredible learning process and I couldn't have asked for a better team to do it with.

Thank you to all my family – Mum, Dad, my partner Phoebe and our daughter, Isabella. As the foundations of my world, I couldn't have written this book, or done any of the things in it, without your unconditional love and support. I hope I can continue to make you proud.

Finally, thank you to everyone that I've had the pleasure of sharing paddocks and pitlanes with for the last fifteen years. Racing attracts a special type of person, and I've been very lucky to work with some amazing ones. Thank you to all of you who've shown your support for this book, I am truly grateful.